DATE DUE

North to Alaska's Shining River

by Hazel Dunaway Berto

the NEW *Bobbs-Merrill* COMPANY, INC.
AN ASSOCIATE OF HOWARD W. SAMS & CO., INC.
Publishers • INDIANAPOLIS • NEW YORK

To My Loved Ones:
my husband—without whose help and encouragement
this book would not have been written—my son,
my daughter and my mother.

North to Alaska's
Shining River

Chapter 1

SLEEP CAME SLOWLY the first night aboard the small government boat *Boxer*. The bewilderment of gentle faces still haunted me. Get married at eighteen? Bury oneself for a year at Yaka, an Eskimo village on Norton Sound at the edge of the Bering Sea? John and I had been hired by the Indian Bureau to teach the Eskimo children. For the remaining weeks of summer we were to help build an orphanage at Blue Ridge, some eighty miles east of Nome, and then go on to the settlement at Yaka before winter began.

The doubts of my mother and father had disturbed me. Yes, both John and I were young and inexperienced. There was only one doubt I did not share: to my parents, John was an adventuresome man they hardly knew. Was it the danger ahead that shook my confidence? What would it be like to spend a year in such a wilderness? The howl of the malemute, the call of wild geese, the roar of a blizzard above the river and trail . . . I pushed away the sheet and reached for the light. Two o'clock. I lay back, overwhelmed by the future. Behind stretched familiar patterns—home, college, friends. Ahead, the unknown.

Only a few weeks ago plans for the coming marriage, the excitement of preparing for such a trip had occupied me. How many loaves of bread could be made from a sack of flour? Should we take canned spinach, canned asparagus? What size woolen socks for John? But now, after warnings, and those troubled looks which were more disturbing than warnings, the separation from those I loved and depended on seemed a momentous event. In the bunk above me was John. He was awake, and I climbed in beside him. He held me close and asked if I was sorry. The minute he spoke I knew I was not.

At Ketchikan we were glad to have a chance to stretch our legs but disappointed to find no ice and snow, no dog teams. We visited the stores, admired huge totem poles, gazed at Deer Mountain, but Ketchikan was much like towns we might have seen in the States.

In a few days the sea roughened. The ship, loaded with freight for Alaska's outposts, rolled heavily, sending dishes scurrying back and forth. John encouraged me to walk the deck in the cold wind, the better to get my sea legs. But I had no sea legs— every roll and pitch sent me staggering. At night, when the panelwork creaked with the strain and paint scrapings sifted to the floor of our cabin, I scrambled out of the bunk and clung to the closed porthole. I vowed that if ever I set foot on the dear earth, nothing would budge me to sea again.

When warm, comparatively calm days finally came, John urged me to leave the cabin and join the other passengers on deck. The friendly Bowens and their boy Sonny; the elderly Tripps and their small Tommy; and young Bertha, a widow, and her daughter Susie. Later Bill, a widower on the way north with his son Bobby, paused beside the chair in which Bertha was sitting. At her unyielding glance he resumed his tour of the deck.

Through the peaceful waters of the Inland Passage the *Boxer* steamed. We lay on blankets to soften the bags of coal and the piles of lumber lashed to the deck. Steep, forested mountains, rising majestically on either side, grew and dimmed. For hours, on edges of shiplap and heaps of shingles, we sat Indian-fashion, singing college songs or becoming silent in the world of silence surrounding the boat. Animals roamed the banks, birds soared overhead, but no human being waved, none saw our passing. The smoke of Petersburg rose from afar. Juneau, tucked in the lee of rising hills, was a town of gold mines and buildings dipping close to the water's edge. We steamed through narrow gorges, unloading freight at remote villages where faces of a few looked up from the wharves. Then, in the shallow Gulf of Alaska, strong winds once more swept the sea into a rage, sending the *Boxer* dipping, swaying and creaking. Bertha, the young and pretty widow, accepted Bill's arm as she went below.

Embarrassed because I was still the worst sailor in the group, I put my hands to white cheeks. John turned with a smile. "Don't fret, Dolly. You're doing all right."

By the time I was able to be on deck once more, Bill and Bertha sat companionably together. Bill's earnest head was close to hers. The children, Bertha's Susie, Bill's Bobby, played near by. St. Michael, Bertha's point of debarkation for Russian Mission on the Yukon, would come soon. In so short a time, could Bill persuade her to go with him? His urgent concern for her emphasized his interest and intention.

The usually aloof Tripps nodded as we neared them.

"This your first journey?" Mr. Tripp's accent was Norwegian. His face bore the heaviness of an older man. His wife, many years younger, was small, with sun-bleached, wispy hair.

We nodded. "We're booked for Yaka," John explained.

"But first we go to Blue Ridge to help build an orphanage for Eskimo children." He looked at their silent faces. "You aren't going there too?"

Mr. Tripp pushed puffy hands through the last wisps of his gray hair. Mrs. Tripp's perpetual frown deepened between sharp eyes.

"We are," she said, "but we hope it isn't too late to make a change."

John said, "I don't understand——"

She interrupted. "We want a village of our own to work with, as we've had in the past." Her glance showed what she thought of our youth. "We're experienced in handling our own natives. We know what to do in emergencies. We know how to barter and how to handle the reindeer herds." Her eyes said, *Do you?*

I looked from her jutting chin to the top of Mr. Tripp's wispy-bald head. Yes, they were more experienced, but I had the impulse to call them hardened to experience. Whatever we lacked, we had much more than they.

The *Boxer* was steaming toward the Aleutian Range. To our left was the green of Kodiak Island. We were following the Alaska Peninsula, near the Valley of Ten Thousand Smokes, the active volcano Mt. Katmai. We'd passed the glaciers of Prince William Sound and the surrounding forests of hemlock and spruce. And Seward, railhead, gateway to the interior. And Anchorage, then a young and growing town. Soon we would enter Unimak Pass and head north again toward Bristol Bay.

The wind was blowing my hair. I'd tied a ribbon around it, and the ribbon made me feel very young. I wrapped my coat closer. A breath of cold air chilled my neck. But it was the disapproval of the Tripps I felt most keenly. Suddenly, with no sound but the chugging of the boat, the splish-splash of the waves against the side, I felt the inadequacy of our youth, the immaturity of our years, as if we were bits of flotsam cast upon unyielding waters.

We left the Tripps and circled the deck once more, feeling their irritation at thwarted plans. "They've not given up," John said. "They still hope someone's mind can be changed."

"I wish I didn't feel so panicky," I said. "I don't know quite why."

We fell silent, thinking of the security of home, of friends, of college, of the familiar things we'd left behind. They were so far away.

John chewed on a matchstick. "I wonder," he said, "how you barter with Eskimos? I thought it sounded easy enough, but the Tripps made me doubtful. And managing reindeer—must be a big job." He was frowning, perplexed. "I thought I could just think of reindeer as so many horses and cows. I guess," he said, grinning suddenly, "we've taken on quite a load!"

King Cove, on the southerly end of the peninsula, was a miniature world of all races. We stared at swarthy faces, high cheekbones, uncut and jagged hair. Even Bertha faltered, experiencing with us a sudden failure of confidence, before she hurried on with Bill; whatever her thoughts, she kept them to herself. Without John to steady me, I'd have been ready to sail right back to the States.

At a cry we turned abruptly, just as a huge black object surfaced and slithered back into the sea.

"Whale!" We were quite unprepared for the magnitude of the glistening body. A spout of water shot into the sky to our left; instantly another great body rose and sank into the depths. Suddenly, as if they tired of their play, the whales were gone.

A deckhand paused at his work, grinning at our awe and delight. "You'll see plenty more ahead. This is their playground. Akutan—that's where you'll see whales."

One more omen that the world we were entering was unlike anything we'd experienced.

Chapter 2

AKUTAN, the whaling station, came to us on the wind. We'd looked into the glacial whiteness of dozens of icebergs, some pinnacled, some worn with their wanderings, some slowly drowning. We'd watched as huge chunks of ice slid into the sea from the Columbia Glacier. We were slowly growing tired of confinement aboard. Akutan would give us a little time ashore.

Long before we tied to the wharf, the new scent came to us. Thousands of seagulls screamed, swooped, landed and took off again from every piling. Boards of the buildings near the wharf were spattered white with their presence.

Stepping warily, we left the boat and went along the wharf to watch a dead whale towed into port.

A bit of whale flesh, so grotesque it seemed a flaw of Mother Nature, lay at our feet. After a tour of the boardwalks John stooped beside the lump of flesh. I didn't want him to touch it. With a pocket knife he sawed off a fragment. "For later inspection," he explained, running with me to the *Boxer*.

And on we steamed. We passed the fishing grounds of Bristol Bay, the tundra in the region of Kuskokwim Bay. Nunivak Island swept by, and the great brush-and-tundra region of the Yukon came closer. Soon Bertha must debark or travel on with

15

Bill. As St. Michael came in sight, John shook his head. "I'm afraid Bill won't make it." It was too much to expect, that in so short a time Bertha would accept him. We walked the deck, looking anxiously for some evidence that Bill had persuaded her. When the boat dropped anchor at St. Michael, Bertha gathered her bags and her child. Long after she had left us, to begin her trek up the Yukon toward Russian Mission, Bill continued his vigil, his smile stilled. The chance that they would meet again was unlikely.

At Unalakleet, where thin vapor rises above the flatland, we turned regretfully to say good-by to the Bowens. "Are you nervous to be landing?" I asked. The *Boxer* pitched, and I clutched my supper plate, wishing desperately that this was Yaka, our own destination.

Mr. Bowen nodded. "After all, Ohio is a long way from the Bering Sea in every sense."

Mrs. Bowen forked into her pie. "You folks are so awfully young. Aren't you a tiny bit scared?"

"Scared?" I echoed. "Of what?"

She looked at Sonny—his bright eyes, his smooth cheeks—and then she straightened the already straight collar of his shirt. "Oh, well," she said, "of nothing, I suppose. I guess there's nothing really. . . ."

Before the meal was done, the ship anchored far offshore. We finished our pie and went up on deck. Adventure, excitement, some bewilderment in the face of a strange land—these we'd felt. But fear had never alarmed me. Now, however, the closer we came the less certain I was of my courage. I didn't know what there was to be frightened of, and this bothered me, but gradually the idea that we were going alone into a wilderness grew more and more disturbing. The same low spirits hovered over the others, even John, as we stared at a vast, flat land where distant vapor rose from the shadows.

Sonny pointed at the shore. "Where's the snow?" he asked. There was no sign of snow. It was late July, and the sun would stay high in the heavens. "And the dog teams!" he cried. "They said there'd be dogs and sleds."

"There will be," John said, "when it's winter again."

As a scow came from the beach, Mr. Tripp explained. "There are no wharves this far north because of the ice, so these boats— lighters, they call them—come out to meet the ships and take passengers and freight to shore."

When boxes, cartons and sacks began filling the barge, John asked, "How come so many?" It looked as if the Bowens had bought out an entire store.

"There may not be another boat in here the rest of the summer. And none at all until next spring. Food, building material, barter, mail—everything the teachers and traders have ordered for themselves, the school, the medicine closet and the natives— everything has to arrive before the freeze." And that explained why the decks had been crowded with stacks of lumber, bags of coal. "Larger ships don't call at all the villages," Mr. Bowen said. "The government boat is the only one that does. You'll understand the need before you leave Alaska."

It was time for the Bowens to say good-by. We felt our throats tighten; we'd grown closer than any of us knew on this journey north. "Take care of yourselves," they said soberly.

The *Boxer* churned up a turbulent backwash. The whistle blasted a final farewell. We watched, waving, as the scow approached the beach and long after the Bowens had been set down on shore. The *Boxer* began to move again. Both John and I had the same impulse. We didn't want to be watching when there was nobody left to see. Slowly, thoughtfully, we went below deck to our cabin.

At last, late one evening, we heard "Yaka!" Suddenly I wanted to be unpacked and settled more than anything in the world. We dropped anchor; while a scow gorged itself with freight, our good spirits returned. "It'll be fine having our supplies here when we come back in September," I said. "But how will we get back?"

Mrs. Tripp's frown softened as she explained. "The government takes care of all that! Before the freeze-up they'll bring you—or someone—back to Yaka!"

"But our clothes!"

"You probably have all you'll need in your suitcases and steamer trunk."

John read my thoughts. "The other trunk is roped, and Lord knows how deep it'll be stored once it reaches shore."

He was right, of course. To hunt at night through tons of supplies for a trunk wasn't possible.

Almost at once we landed in half-darkness. We stood looking into a sea of shadowy faces, and then someone took our arms, guiding us up the narrow boardwalks into a huge storage building whose ceiling vanished in the dim light. Boxes and cartons were carted in, and somewhere in this cavern lay our year's supply of food and clothing.

Eskimo women, with babes on their backs, came over and touched my face, and their smiles broadened in their round, brown faces. You are young, they were trying to tell me. They pointed at John. How big and handsome he was! We smiled back at them. We had hoped to see more of our future home but in the darkness there was little to see. Disappointed, we took one more look at the place where our belongings would await us and boarded the launch to return to the *Boxer*.

Bill had been watching us take supplies ashore. John gripped his shoulder in passing and said something meant to be cheerful. I closed our cabin door, glad to be with John, and wishing Bertha were here to comfort Bill and his son. For life at Teller was a land of silence, of endlessness. You had to have someone. Dog teams, fishing, hunting, and driving a sled could never answer the call for companionship during the bitter nights.

We hove to in Golovin Bay after twenty-one days on board ship. "Just a few hours up the Fish River, then solid ground for us!" John exclaimed, eying the faint shore.

We crowded into the launch. As it drew near the beach, all the village dogs howled in a bedlam of noise. Children and adults swarmed around us. There were little girls with red bandanas tied around their dark heads and little boys with black slanting eyes who studied us intently. And squaw men with their Eskimo wives. I thought involuntarily of Bill.

Beyond, old frame buildings, sagging on their foundations. In every yard chained dogs howling from their dusty pits. And mosquitoes. Everywhere we turned, they swarmed around us. At first we swatted them, we swatted each other, we pulled our collars up, and always we scratched. Great lumps rose on our arms, our legs, our necks, our foreheads. They bit through shirts and blouses, they found bare spots at the back of our necks. We swatted them, not knowing the futility of it, and wondered how we were to travel upriver. Then Mr. and Mrs. Rance rushed toward us.

"I'm village superintendent, and this is my wife, matron at the orphanage—when we finish it." As they shook our hands, her bright eyes examined my weary face.

"You've had quite a trip," Mrs. Rance said, "and a hard one on that poky boat. But you won't have long to wait now; you'll soon be there."

I thanked her. She was about fifty, I imagined. She was guessing my age too. "You're the youngest we've had. Well, we like them young, don't we, Charles?" She didn't wait for her husband's answer but took my arm and started toward a building she spoke of as Sam's Café. "We'll all eat here before we start upriver in the launch."

The café had been built in the days of the Gold Rush. We crossed its slanting porch and settled at one of the battered tables covered with oilcloth. We met the owner, a white man married to a native. He too was a relic of the Gold Rush, with weathered skin, brawny physique, complete alienation from stateside life as we knew it.

As we sat down, we became aware of the eyes of all the children who had followed us. They stood on the porch, peering in. I leaned toward John. "I've never seen so many brown eyes."

He looked around at the silent children, at the mothers with babies tied on their backs, at the dogs scurrying everywhere. "I feel," he said, "like an intruder from another planet. I'll bet they've even counted the hairs on our heads!"

When Sam brought our dinner, Mr. Rance said, "Reindeer steak. You'll like it."

I looked at it dubiously. The meat was darker than any I'd ever eaten; its odor different from any I was accustomed to. I looked up and found Sam's Eskimo wife watching us, her dark face warm from the cookstove.

John cut into his steak gingerly, and I watched as he took his first bite. "Gamy," he said, "but tender."

I tried a piece, but the odor was too strong for me. Sam's wife looked disappointed, so I made a meal of the potatoes and canned peas, homemade bread and butter and pie with strong coffee. Smiling at last, she backed into the kitchen.

At the beach we boarded the launch for the last miles of our long journey. In order to find the channel up Fish River, we, with the Rances, the Tripps and two Eskimos, headed out into the bay to avoid the danger of grounding in the shallow, ever-changing sands. It was the first day of August, and the early afternoon sun was warm on our backs. I shed my coat, and John slipped off his sweater.

"I can't help wondering what's ahead," John said as the village faded from sight. "We've been on our way so long, home seems like a dream."

I nodded. "Like a dream. I can't help wondering how we'll make out." We turned to watch the Tripps sitting alone, un-smiling, their faces expressing complete dissatisfaction.

"They aren't reconciled," John said. "They're still hoping to have their own village."

"Their faces are so—so determined," I said, feeling a chill of apprehension. "I feel too young and incapable—and so com-pletely tongue-tied—when I'm around her. Do they blame us for their being sent to this place, do you suppose?"

"How could they?" John said. "We never laid eyes on them before the trip began. If we drew Yaka instead of Blue Ridge, we can't help it!"

"This must be wonderful hunting," I said to Mukuk, one of the guides.

Mukuk's face lighted up. "Good big hunting! Lots of ducks and geese!"

"And fishing?"

The grin broadened as Mukuk nodded vigorously. "Lots of fish all the time—spring, winter, summer."

John came back to me, puzzled. "Now how do you suppose they catch fish with the river frozen solid?" He wondered if

Mukuk was making fun of us. Fishing through ice three or four feet thick?

The boat swerved first to one bank and then the other, keeping within the channel. Riffles just ahead barely covered the rocks, yet we were headed straight toward them.

"The river," Mukuk explained, "is very shallow sometimes. We have hard time, many times. Maybe we have to get out and walk along the bank part way."

"But the scows—what do they do?"

"They bring horses on the barge. When shallow water comes, horses get off the barge and from the bank pull the barge over the riffles. Then horses get back on the barge."

John stared at the river. He was imagining what it must have been like when miners by the tens of thousands came up this winding river to the gold fields of Ophir Creek.

But how could they? Council was a long way upstream. And there were hundreds of houses to bring lumber for; there were tons of food and clothing and supplies to bring upriver. Furniture for hotels, houses, cafés. We sat silent, sensing the struggle of the past and the romance of it.

John looked ahead. "Dolly, if we're still here in the spring, let's take a trip to Council and Ophir Creek."

We saw it first as a blur on the banks of the river, this new village where we were to live until winter; where the gold miners stopped on their way to the fields; where the old Wild Goose Warehouse stood at the landing. Native houses stretched in sprawling shapes along the shore and in ragged clusters on the hill at the foot of the white-capped mountain. From everywhere figures in cotton parkas and bright kerchiefs came running. Jumping from the boat to the landing, we found ourselves the object of every eye. Excited chattering and curious glances meant one thing: we were the new teachers, maybe? But we only shook our heads, for Mr. Rance had warned us that changes might be made in our plans. We couldn't be sure where the next weeks would find us. I followed the others on a path to the left, climbing up, up, past the towering warehouse, the school, until we looked down over the shining river and far to the surrounding hills.

Before us the white-tipped mountain snuggled houses at its feet—the trim, yellow house that was the superintendent's; the long, low, inviting cottage that was the nurse's; and finally the red, square house that looked like a neglected orphan. Its two windows overlooked the river and the door stood ajar. At that moment its gauntness seemed to belong to the wilderness, and instantly I loved it, for all its starkness. After all, this was the first house John and I could call our own.

Someone came from the door of the small red house and stood motionless on the rough porch.

Mr. Rance's droning voice broke in. "This house will be for the teachers after the orphanage is built. But for now it must be shared with the Swens." And he nodded toward the couple coming down the steps.

Mrs. Swen, still in her twenties, beamed and put her arm around my waist. "We came in on the early boat," she said, "because Jerry wanted to get started on the orphanage."

And where, I wondered, were we to find a niche in a world so suddenly complex? Here we were, yet we really weren't here at all. Our baggage, our food, some of our clothing and most of our personal items lay on a beach far down the coast. More of our baggage and some of our clothes were on the beach at Golovin Bay. The rest we clung to on this narrow path, with mosquitoes buzzing us and strangers holding our hands.

Mrs. Rance smiled. "We all need some good hot coffee." She squeezed my arm knowingly. "The coffeepot's always on in Alaska, you know."

Mrs. Rance clung doggedly to my arm. I looked back. John was coming too. And behind him trudged the rest of the colony, with Mr. Tripp speaking earnestly to Mr. Rance. We crowded into the yellow house where the Rances lived. I edged closer to John as Mrs. Rance disappeared into the kitchen.

"Have a chair," invited Mr. Rance, as he introduced Miss Charles, the nurse. Her white hair was combed severely back from a heavy face and wrinkles etched the folds of her jaw. As she shook my hand she looked through her bifocals so intently I felt blood rush to my face. "You're very young," she finally concluded, and then she went to John, looking up at his six feet two. "And you can do a lot to help me be more comfortable!" I watched her fold her arms across her heavy bosom; after that I turned for my cup of coffee, hoping that I'd never have to cross her, and resenting the way she had all but appropriated John.

At last the Swens rose. The coffee had made us welcome, but we needed a place to hang our coats and remove our traveling clothes.

Out in the yard I looked toward the slope where the orphanage was to be built. All would have to be cleared and leveled before even the foundation could be laid. The weeks ahead looked endless, with crowded living conditions and lack of privacy. Not for days would we know where we'd be spending the winter. In the meantime, our supplies—the eggs, potatoes, the bacon—must wait where they were.

John turned back, and I heard the excitement in his voice. "Think you can climb that mountain with me, Dolly?" And with his enthusiasm, the thoughts of the coming weeks with him caught my spirits and sent them skyrocketing.

I took his hand, aware of the adventure of the present, as Mrs. Swen opened the door of the red house and ushered us inside.

The big wood heater faced us in the living room; to our right under the window was a couch; beyond was the kitchen. To our left was the bedroom door and to its left the tinest organ I had ever seen. Its keyboard wasn't complete, and it was scarred with age, but I touched its pitted keys with delight. A friend at last! Here was something I knew well. Here, squatting so comfortingly, was the soothing spirit of home. As I touched the keyboard, the red house was an orphan no longer.

The glow I felt made me discount the iron bedstead, the sagging spring and mattress, in the room which would be our only refuge. The glow carried me through the storeroom, filled now with the Swens' food, and the second bedroom. Beyond that, in the kitchen, the huge black wood range burned low. A table and chairs stood under the window.

"Luckily I brought some odd curtains." Mrs. Swen smiled. "They help to brighten the place." Cooling on the counter were freshly baked bread and cinnamon rolls, their fragrance making me instantly hungry. Mrs. Swen handed me a roll. "You look starved. Go take off your coat and relax while I peel potatoes for dinner. Tomorrow will be time enough to help me."

In our bedroom I took off my coat and slumped to the bed. John came in. "We were looking over the orphanage site," he said. "It's going to be a big job getting it built in time before we have to get back to Yaka."

I propped myself against the bedstead. "Did you hear anything more about the Tripps' assignment?"

"Nothing. But they don't intend to stay here if they can help it. Besides, he's an old man to be working on this sort of job."

"They have their own ideas on how to run a village—she told me that often enough."

"So do the Rances, I'm sure of that," John said. "Well, let's find the wash pan and get some of this travel dust off."

By the time we'd washed, we were hungry again. Mrs. Swen served from the kettles on the stove—reindeer steak, potatoes, gravy, canned vegetables. And she supplied bread and brine-butter, rolls and peaches.

"The potatoes won't last much longer," she said, "unless we get a late shipment on the last boat. I'll hate to see them gone."

"The natives are predicting an early freeze," said Mr. Swen.

"That means no more fresh eggs when these are gone. Nor fruit."

"I suppose by the time we get back to our potatoes and eggs—or they get to us—they'll be spoiled," John said.

"In Alaska," said Mrs. Swen, "you get used to that. The main thing is, did you bring plenty of dried potatoes and eggs, canned milk, butter and coffee?"

"They told us in Seattle that we could get some milk from reindeer, but we bought a case just to be sure."

Mr. Swen snorted. "Did they really tell you that? Why, that's positively ridiculous!"

His wife said, "You'll just have to go down to Golovin and order more, that's all. The price is the worst—about twenty-four dollars a case up here. But you must do it before the freeze, if you stay."

"Twenty-four dollars!" I said. Why, we didn't have five dollars! John had worked all the weeks between college and sailing time in order to buy my wedding ring and our few necessities. We hadn't worried at all, for all our expenses were to be paid and there would be nothing to buy or any place to buy it.

Only once had we wished there was a little more in the kitty. On the way up we'd seen candy in Ketchikan—chocolate drops —and we'd suddenly wanted chocolate more than anything else in the world. We compromised on a sack of jelly beans and the price we had to pay had subtracted immeasurably from our enjoyment.

"I'll have to telegraph for more money as soon as I have a month's pay coming," John said.

"You'll need some for parkas and mukluks and mittens," Mr. Swen reminded us. "Or you can pay for them in coffee."

I felt for and pressed John's foot under the table. The thought of our having more coffee than we needed made me laugh. We had brought just five pounds of coffee; we rarely drank it; but in these few days we had seen gallons of the stuff on every stove. Fifty pounds would have been closer to the amount we would need up here! Already we could see that our order from Golovin would be an expensive one.

Daylight faded as we finished dinner, but darkness did not come early. After washing the dishes, John and I strolled out. But we didn't stay long, for thousands of mosquitoes descended upon us, buzzed us at every step, zoomed in at every swat. We turned and ran for shelter, thankful for screens. We went to bed in daylight. We were so weary that the pillows felt soft and the mattress like down. The dogs in the village were howling and voices of playing children rose on the summer air. John reached over and pulled me closer. Above our heads a mosquito buzzed. We both lay tense, waiting for the bite. Then John lashed out viciously and hit his face with a terrific thud. That broke the tenseness and we both giggled uncontrollably. When one of us stopped it was only to swat another buzzer, which promptly set us off into another spasm of laughter. Finally, in desperation, we hid our heads under the sheet and, too tired to wrestle longer with mosquitoes and the hiccoughs, fell asleep.

Chapter 3

THE BUILDING of the orphanage now became the first order of the day. As John, the villagers and Mr. Tripp labored along with Mr. Swen, the ground was cleared, the brush piled and burned. Every noon found the men dusty, tired and starved. Every evening found another space leveled. They hoped to pour foundations before freezing weather and beat the deadline of school, when Mr. Swen would be left with only the villagers to help.

Life took on all the aspects of pioneering as Mrs. Swen and I cooked, scrubbed and cleaned. Clothes were scrubbed on a washboard in a zinc tub, then boiled in a copper boiler. Ironing was done with heavy, black flatirons heated on the range. With a broom, we scrubbed floors heartily and often.

Bread was set at night and baked the next day, each batch furnishing us with a starter for the next. There were endless hours of kneading, mixing, rolling for cinnamon rolls, pinching for dinner rolls. Pies, cakes, doughnuts and cookies were made almost daily to keep up with the ever-hungry men. Not until Sunday did the work ease, and even then the chores must go on but at a slower pace. Cooked mush was our staple breakfast food, but the sight of condensed milk spreading over its surface appalled me. The eggs toward the end of the crate became increasingly strong and smelly. But as the weeks went by, the milk seemed tasty and the eggs became precious.

After each day's work, when the hills were hazed in purple shadows, John and I strolled down the path toward the river and beyond to the village. All through the hours of the day we were never alone; hiking along the path hand in hand gave us the privacy we missed. Not even the mosquitoes deterred us.

"Have you heard any news?" I asked one evening, and John shook his head.

"I know that Tripp is—well, marking time, perhaps. I suppose there are ways to force a decision—or to change one."

We passed the school and the village, which scarcely covered two blocks, and after that we followed the bank of the river or hiked toward the slope of the mountain or, reluctantly, turned homeward. There were no roads, for there was no reason to travel them, and there was no other village for at least forty miles. I confided that I'd tried my hand with the bread that day, and John explained the progress of the building I so anxiously watched. We discussed the conferences that took place daily between Mr. Rance and Mr. Tripp. Now and then John shook his head at the anger he had seen on their faces as they parted.

"Being unsure is the hardest," he said, "if there is such a *hardest* thing after we've planned."

"We'll have to know soon. They can't wait much longer to send one of us away."

The village life intrigued us, haunting us with its battered, simple complacency and the growing feud.

Tina was the first to greet us. She was the woman-leader of the village, and we were aware of it in some intangible way as she held our hands in hers. *"Qua Ka!"* she said softly. Her round, ruddy face opened like a big sunflower beneath braided black hair.

Her house was swept clean; in a corner, rolled out of the way, were beds of reindeer skin; a rickety stove held a stained, chipped coffeepot; tiny windows let in the dull light; hanging on nails were parkas, mukluks and guns. A few cracked dishes lay on a shelf by the stove.

John stooped a bit in order to clear the low door, and Tina laughed in glee. "You so tall," she said, "not like Jim."

Inside, squatting on the bare floor, were the children and Jim, sitting around a single bowl of cooked fish. "Oh," said John, backing toward the door, "you're having dinner."

"Uh-huh," Jim said, dipping into the bowl. The children sat silent, their big eyes friendly.

John touched Tina's heavy shoulder. "We'll come back some other time."

She nodded. "You come back."

We strolled out over the hard-packed ground. Children ran to windows or stopped in their play as we passed. Some of the boys were playing with a big skin ball, throwing it back and forth while others tried to intercept it. Men sat in doorways, looking over the river as they mended nets. They looked up as we passed, grinned and said, *"Qua Ka!"* We went toward Ivory Pete's open door, turning our heads a bit at the peculiar odor that met us. Ivory Pete lived alone, bent with frugal years and a lame, tubercular hip, fashioning ivory carvings with the aid of a spinning gadget he had rigged up. We saw him stooped over this crude machine, his thin face lined with effort, his hair long over his ears.

"Let's go in," John suggested. The odor was like a curtain of fog as we entered. "Breathe shallow," John warned.

Ivory Pete grinned toothlessly. Like many of the older natives, he spoke almost no English. He showed us letter openers, pointing pridefully to the pictures of Blue Ridge cut on the handles, and penholders carved with dog teams, bear and deer. Napkin holders, lockets and trinkets were stained with the juice of berries. After we had shown our delight, we backed out of the curtain of smell.

Ivory Pete looked downcast that we had not bought something. "We'll come back," John told him.

Outside, we breathed deeply and well, bringing air to the bottoms of our lungs. "Whew," said John. "We don't know what it means to be poor. Or live a life of simplicity."

"One broken stove, a box, a shelf, a reindeer skin for a bed," I said, "but his craft gives him something to be proud of." A thought struck me. "But with so few people here to buy what he makes and almost no traffic upriver, how does he manage to live?"

"He does," said John as we continued.

We saw another open door. No one stood in it, but as we passed we caught a glimpse of a staring face that reached to our hearts. It was the whitest face I'd ever seen, with cheekbones standing high and lean and bleached. Great hollow eyes in the skeletonlike face, forehead like parchment—I clutched John's arm and looked away from the dying face, feeling sick with the distress that comes at the first sight of nearing death.

The next day I went with Miss Charles, the nurse, on her village calls, and many times after that. During these visits my feelings of pity for the sick and dying deepened as tuber-

culosis took its toll. I watched Miss Charles give out aspirin for
sedatives, and I understood how little could be done for these
afflicted. Special diets were impossible without the necessary
food; isolation was hopeless in one-room huts. So these smiling,
cheerful people ate, slept and finally died in a single little room.

Miss Charles, in her largeness, seemed to fill every hut she
entered, and her booming voice that tried to be cheerful filled
the villagers with fear. She exploded at the sight of an unswept
house and berated them when they had not remembered to make
broth for the sick.

The skeleton-white face always filled me with awe and sorrow. Each week the bony hands grew larger; the woman's arms
lay translucent. Often her legs were drawn up and the sight
of her withered, wasted brown body filled me with misery.

"How much longer must she suffer?" I asked Miss Charles,
but the nurse could only shake her head.

"All over Alaska," she said bitterly, "they're dying like this.
And they'll keep on dying unless a miracle comes along—and
miracles don't happen in Alaska."

I thought of the orphanage rising slowly. "Orphanages aren't
enough," I said. "They're only a result of these stricken families."

She looked at me and nodded. "We know that. But how can
we hospitalize all of Alaska?"

Later that evening John and I stopped to watch Ivory Pete
at his wheel; we stopped again to watch work on a half-mended
fish net, and then we turned homeward, passing open doorways
where the living would die.

"Such a waste of life!" John said.

"But simply knowing the waste won't help, Miss Charles
says."

We looked back at the village, now darkening with twilight, its sounds ebbing with the day. "Two of us can't do much, but even our efforts might ease somebody's suffering."

Work on the orphanage progressed more rapidly. The days were hard, wearying and long. Everyone realized that each day brought winter and the freeze nearer, and Mr. Swen knew it more surely than the rest. "We've got to be in the new building by the first week of September," he said, and we bent every effort toward that goal. The framework soon pushed into the sky; the roof and the siding followed. And every day we wondered about the future.

And then suddenly the decision was made. It was in John's disappointed face as he came down the hill from the building at lunchtime. It was in Mr. Tripp's buoyant step as he took his place at the table.

That afternoon Mrs. Swen packed a few supplies. "You'll soon be using your own," she said, pushing her hair from her forehead. "And I hear you'll be staying here instead of returning to Yaka."

I nodded. "We did so want to go back."

She folded some woolen underwear, her face cheering in its happiness. "We're tickled to death you're staying," she said. "You've no idea how difficult it is to keep peace among such a group through the winter months—we know from experience. Every little thing becomes a major catastrophe when there's no one else to visit but the same two or three couples. Someone's bound to feel picked on or left out or trammeled. It's very queer."

"How ridiculous!" I said. "Why, it should be just the opposite up here, when we're so alone. Do you really think——"

She glanced up. "It's a long time until spring."

I looked out at the quiet river and the blue-tinged hills. I didn't want to believe the possibility, yet there was no denying that we, a group of strangers, lived helplessly at one another's doors.

John laughed when I told him about it later. "What on earth could there be to fight over up here?" Yet his face clouded momentarily. Was he beginning to label each of our neighbors? For already we'd seen temper, stubbornness and a false and petty pride.

I changed the subject. "Will the Swens be able to move into the new building by the seventh of September?"

We sat on the high bank overlooking the river, with mosquito netting covering us. "That's the way it looks now. The remaining inside work can be finished after they move in."

"I sometimes think the seventh will never come," I told him, holding my knees close, "and I'm sure Mrs. Swen does too!"

"Are we going to have enough food for the winter?"

"I've been going over the list again. If we eat peaches one day in ten, and carrots one day in seven, and everything else accordingly, maybe we will."

John grinned and shooed the mosquitoes from his hat brim. "There's a challenge for a bride! With all the dried and evaporated things you've had to learn to use . . ." He sailed a large pebble toward the water. "But we'll manage. It may mean a little leanness and toughness and a stiff upper lip, but it'll take more than that to beat us down."

The rock plunked into the river. "Mrs. Rance said the Eskimos use lard on their bread instead of butter. Sounds horrible, but in a pinch——"

On the seventh, true to their plans, the Swens moved into the orphanage. As their supplies moved out of the red house, ours moved in, having arrived from Yaka on the boat which carried the Tripps away.

It was great fun setting up housekeeping for the first time, and John and I stood back admiring the shelves in the storage room.

"Looks good enough to eat," John said, gloating. "How about a dish of pears and a cooky?" He put his arm around my shoulders, but he wasn't seeing the full shelves before us. He was feeling relaxation after the strain of close living.

Taking a can of pears and a box of cookies from the shelf, he led me to the kitchen. Some of the tension had eased from his face. "You know, it's the strangest thing. For weeks I've just been waiting for the time when I could go in there and get something to eat if I felt like it. I've never had that craving before!"

I opened the can of pears. "I've had exactly the same feeling. Just seeing the Swens' box of dried prunes on the shelf made me drool—and I've never drooled over prunes before."

John threw back his head and laughed. He scooped up the first bite of pears, then said, "What's more, we'll splurge. We'll get out the prunes and dried figs."

"No more drooling," he said, reaching inside the box and bringing out a prune.

"At college we used to feel this way," I remarked, "but when we did, we simply went to the store and bought our craving. But here . . ." I chewed on two prunes, savoring them.

"Never again will a fig taste so delicious," John declared.

Getting ready for bed was pure luxury. We lazed around and talked aloud instead of in the hushed whispers we had used when the Swens were there.

"Will you have a drink of water?" John yelled, dipping the metal dipper into our own pail of water. "This is living," he said, quieter now, "even if we do finally come down to beans and bread." He looked at me questioningly. "Do we have enough flour to keep us in bread for the duration?"

We went back and counted the sacks of flour again, but we still didn't know whether we had ordered enough. "I've never baked bread before," I faltered. "How do I know how much flour it takes for a year?"

"Well, we can eat pilot crackers like the sourdough does in an emergency. They're so hard and dry, one bite will last a long, long time!"

The next morning was even nicer. We decided to have the luxury of evaporated eggs and toast. The eggs, in fine flakes, had to soak a while, and then be beaten, much like scrambled eggs. The first bite left us downcast.

John bit into his toast. "They don't taste quite right," he said.

I watched the water ooze slowly from the eggs.

"Maybe there are other ways to cook them," he suggested, pushing the lumps cautiously, but I couldn't see how else you could cook eggs dissolved in water.

"I'll ask Mrs. Rance," I said. "She'll know."

But she didn't know any other way to cook them. "I still have a few fresh ones," she confided, "although they are getting a little old now."

I understood completely. I'd eaten my last "fresh" egg some days before, and I could still remember the odor. The evaporated eggs were preferable; they had their odor too, but it was not that of a rotten egg.

With school opening in the middle of October, recipes for the busy days ahead occupied much of my time, especially those for fish, fowl and venison—to be our main source of meat this year. Although cookbooks were notably short of such recipes, I did not give up the hunt. Goose with dressing; duck with onion, with raisins, with dried apples, with oysters—conscientiously I copied them all, even though I was sure the result would be strong and gamy. Reindeer meat does not change color or texture, but we learned in time neither to sniff nor to savor. We ate it, realizing that it was, like an only dress, not to be discarded.

Our five pounds of coffee had dwindled to three, for here too our appetites had changed. Without reindeer milk as a source of supplement, our quota of canned milk had been depleted.

"I asked Mr. Rance to bring milk from Golovin on his next trip with the launch," John said. He balanced a pole across his shoulders, from which hung two buckets of water he'd carried from the river below.

"Aren't reindeer ever milked?"

"Not around here. Can you imagine going out to the herd, roping a mamma deer and trying to milk her? I wouldn't want to try it. Right now I haven't the faintest desire to taste one more new thing, have you?"

I shook my head and watched as he went down the path with the dangling buckets. He was lean and his face was tanned from the weeks of sun. I wished suddenly that my family could know the happiness we felt in spite of these minor hardships.

Chapter 4

A FEW DAYS later a great shout of "Seal! Seal!" came from the village. Women turned to look upriver; men eased into their kayaks. We followed; this was the first time we had watched our Eskimo neighbors hunt. A dark object far out in the current rose and disappeared hurriedly. The men bent to their paddles. The kayaks crept closer. A great silence hung over the river. Suddenly there was a rush, a closing-in, a shattering volley of shots. Men strove for the seal to a chorus of excited yells from shore. Rarely did a seal come so far upriver, bringing meat and oil to their doors.

Tina, waiting patiently for the kill—the butchering was her duty—was sharpening the half-moon blade of a bone-handled knife.

At last the seal was brought ashore. Skillfully now, Tina slit open the seal's belly, revealing the fat lying close. Piece by piece she carved each man's share. Finally nothing was left but the blood, the bones, the fat and the skin.

She drank some of the warm blood from a bowl and handed little Ella a bone to suck on. "This skin will make boots and a parka that rain and water will not come through." She wiped her greasy hands. "You see this?" She held up the bowl of blood. "This makes good soup, good food. And this fat—he is good for eating all the time." She cleaned the intestine, which also would be eaten. "Sometimes we make big feast down on the beach. Sometimes we get *oogruck* [bearded seal] and we cook him for all the people." She nodded vigorously. "We make big fire on beach. All people come. Nobody work. Everybody stay until *oogruck* is gone."

John and I turned homeward. "Just like one big family, only more so," John said.

We passed the window of the dying face, the open door where Ivory Pete lived and worked. The dogs, chained close to their posts, leaped up at us, snarling and yapping and howling at our backs. The mosquitoes hadn't forgotten us either, and they buzzed incessantly. We passed the Wild Goose Warehouse and strolled on up the hill past the white-windowed schoolhouse to the house perched on the bank. John opened the door.

"I haven't any blood or fat to offer you," he said, "but if you're hungry, I can offer you such lowly things as figs and prunes."

"Perhaps being out of coffee and milk and a little low on other things isn't so tragic after all," I said. I poured hot water from the kettle to the wash basin. We washed carefully.

"You know—" John wiped his hands—"I feel as if we'd come to an unreal land—as if home with all its conveniences were a millennium away. Until now, I never realized how isolated the Eskimos live. Why, aside from what they've heard from the teachers, the missionaries and a few miners, they have no idea of the world beyond this river."

I moved to the table. "Sometimes it makes me remember what Dad said—what would we do in this place if one of us were sick or dying or in need of surgery?"

He followed me to the couch in the living room. "Or——"

There was a little silence. "I know," I said. "If I were going to have a baby."

He put his arms around me. "We'd find a way," he said, "just as the pioneers did coming West."

We'd have to, I thought.

Mr. Rance knocked at the door. "I brought the milk and coffee and the extra butter we had." Inside, he warmed his hands over the big stove and smiled his thin-lipped smile. "School opens in a few weeks. Looks as though we'll have snow by then. Maybe the freeze, too."

"We'll have to order parkas and mukluks," John said, coming to the stove. "Plain woolies just aren't enough."

"I know," I said, shivering a bit at the new coldness. "It makes me dread going to the schoolhouse tomorrow when we get things organized."

The next day we visited the building. A movable partition made two rooms, and a single huge stove squatted at the front. There were blackboards on either side of the stove.

John examined the books skeptically. "Not exactly what the college recommended," he said, leafing through a ragged arithmetic book, "but they'll have to do."

There were cards with *run* and *jump* and *hop* printed on them. "Do you suppose they'll understand the difference between *jump* and *run?*" I asked.

John grinned. "Every time you hold up the card *hop* you must hop to show them."

"And in your room," I said, "when you teach words like *choo-choo* and *chug-chug,* you'll have to play train, for they've never seen trains!"

John closed the partition that divided the room. "When I hear a rabbit going *hop-hop-hop* in your room, I'll send in the fourth graders to watch."

"And when the train goes laboring up the hill, I'll see that mine have grandstand seats in your room."

At college we had learned enough, we thought, but no one had trained us to meet the obstacles we saw in the days ahead.

We left the building arm in arm. Somehow, the warmth of each gave faith and courage to the other, and we knew that come what may, help when needed lay beyond the partition.

As we turned homeward, Ali, a swarthy, educated half-Russian—sometimes substitute teacher in the school—hailed us. His broad, amiable smile revealed strong, white teeth.

"You busy?" he asked.

When we looked at his face, darkened and rough, a vision of his hut with its sagging porch, its reindeer skin beds in single file on a raised platform came back to us. There were Stasha, his Eskimo wife, heavy again with child, and their six children, handsome, alert, intelligent.

Ali interrupted our thoughts. "School pretty soon now, eh?"

"Next week." John grinned. "Will we have many pupils?"

"Maybe forty. Maybe some old ones too. Like me."

John stared. "You?" At Ali's nod John said, "Come on up to the house."

Ali came inside and sat down. He smiled at our bewilderment. "Maybe," he suggested, "I teach you Eskimo and you teach me fractions in arithmetic."

"Fractions?"

"You see," he explained, "the government hires me sometimes to teach, but I cannot teach fractions. So I thought——"

John said, "We'll be glad to help you if we can. We'll start as soon as you wish. Learning Eskimo will be a job for us."

"All Eskimo language is not the same," Ali said. "That is because natives do not travel to distant villages, and because they do not have an alphabet."

"Do you think we can learn all their sounds?" I asked.

Ali smiled. "Here are a few to try," he said. The sounds were very strange. "I will teach you," he said.

He came the next evening for his first lesson, and after John had shown him the meaning of halves, thirds and fourths, he explained to us the words meaning *dog, snow* and *rain*. We learned that one word might mean a phrase or an entire sentence, and that trying to imitate Ali brought fantastic noises from our throats.

"I'll write them down," I volunteered, "so that we can memorize them." But when I tried to syllabilize and accent the words, I couldn't untangle sounds combining a *c* and a *t* with the throaty sounds of *g* thrown in.

The evening was pleasantly rewarding, and Ali was pleased to learn fractions. For weeks we kept up our classes. Ali came regularly and worked hard between classes, but he was a bit discouraged with us as pupils. Daily we wrestled with the throaty sounds, but the gutturals didn't come out as they should. By the time Ali had mastered his simple fractions we were still struggling with our earliest words, so when his lessons were finished it seemed useless for us to continue. Only the months ahead in the village would teach us. Ali's visits, however, helped us understand better the Eskimo pattern of living; and having him as one of our first friends was a great reward in itself.

As soon as John rang the bell on the first school morning, parka-clad children appeared at the door, their cheeks rosy from the chill air. When the nine o'clock bell echoed from the top of the building, the little children followed the example of the older ones and sat quietly. After greeting them, John passed out worn songbooks and I sat down at the old piano. We discovered that first morning how dearly they loved music and rhythm, and this gave us the bond of understanding we sorely needed. By recess the excitement of new pencils, paper and books broke through their reserve. They crowded around my desk, smiling shyly or begging for any odd job I could think of for them to do. At noon when we left for lunch, they loitered in the yard.

John held my elbow. "How was your first half-day?" he teased. He knew of my nervousness these past few weeks.

"Even in the States," I answered, shivering in the cloudy cold, "the very first day is terrorizing."

"But when you say *hop* they know what it means," he teased, opening the door and grinning.

"All the time I was playing games and wondering what they thought of the Mulberry Bush, I kept listening to you tell how Columbus proved the earth was round, and somehow, just hearing your voice was comforting!"

We washed our hands, opened a can of tomato soup and set out the berry pie. "I'm starved," John said, pushing more wood into the range and tasting the soup for hotness every moment or two. "Perhaps we should open two cans of soup!"

I shook my head. "One can of soup every six days, remember?" I hunted the loaf I'd baked the night before. "I'll make toast—that's more filling than crackers, and we can each have one tablespoon of jam."

As we rose from our hasty lunch, John said suddenly, "Look, Dolly!" Far across the school and village the air shook itself gently, loosing a blur of fluttering snowflakes, bringing grayness to the skies, to the horizon. Riverbanks disappeared; rooftops whitened. A breeze whipped the thickening shawl.

At the close of the school day the ground was covered. John poked the fire and we settled ourselves at the window, watching as the silence came and the grayness gradually faded into darkness. Somewhere in the village dogs howled at their chains; lights around us glimmered yellow.

School had been in session a few days. "Just think," said John, finishing his lunch, "in the States, they've got every teaching aid—even to eager supervisors! Here we have to get by as best we can."

I stacked the soiled plates. "Miss Jones at the college would raise a distressed eyebrow if she could see the way I teach words and numbers! Little did she know how I'd be forced to mutilate her *methods*."

"My greatest problem is making a world they can't even imagine come alive," John said.

At the school John kicked snow from his boots. "I can't even find words to explain some of the lessons because they've no experiences with which to associate such things."

We talked again at the end of the day. "I've just got to put some words on the board for tomorrow and get more pictures ready." I leaned wearily against the scarred desk.

John put away the books. He had to carry water from the river. And the firewood needed replenishing. As he left, the bitter cold rushed through the door, and down below ice stretched out across the river. Closing the door, I went back to the dim room, feeling the dull ache, the fatigue of a busy day.

I worked for an hour, but dinner was yet to prepare. Clutching my coat tightly, I closed the door of the school. Outside, the cold evening air penetrated my high boots and thin coat. My breath formed clouds, and my face felt tight. Shivering, I stepped onto the porch, kicked snow from the boots, thankful for a blazing fire within and a chance for a moment's peace before starting dinner. As I reached the door, it opened abruptly and John stood in the yellow light. He drew me to the warmth of the stove and the old rocker.

"Give me your coat—" he eased it from my shoulders—"and relax!"

Holding the stiff boots toward the fire, I lay back and closed my eyes. The warmth crept to my fingers and toes, and, leaning back, I wiggled under its magic spell. A faint step made me open my eyes. John came cautiously, stealthily, carrying a lighted birthday cake, his eyes aglow in the wavering light.

And then I remembered. Today I was nineteen. He held up a hand to stop my rush. Then he began to sing, "Happy birthday to you." And suddenly I turned from the voice, from that gentle face, to the old rocker, trying to keep the weight pressing on my chest from lifting to my throat, to keep the tears from scalding my cheeks. He put aside the cake, pulling me to his lap, brushing away the tears, rocking me slowly. I looked at the pink candles burning low. "You made me a cake! That's why you came home early."

He nodded and put his head against mine. "It has everything in it—dried eggs, too. We probably won't be able to eat it."

I smiled. "We've got to eat it!" I rose and blew out the candles and noticed the straw flowers. "Why, where did these come from?"

"Home," John said. "Your mother gave them to me before we left. They're the only kind that would last till your birthday."

"And the candles, too. You didn't forget a thing . . ."

After a moment we went into the kitchen. He had fixed creamed salmon, toast and a salad of canned fruit, and beside my plate was an ivory letter opener.

"From Ivory Pete's." I picked it up. "And that's Blue Ridge etched on the handle."

"It's to remember this village and this day," John said. "Here, you're the guest of honor. Sit down and be served your banquet." And, with a flourish, he sat me down and filled my plate with creamed salmon.

And when we were ready for the cake, it was the best cake I'd ever eaten. The little holes didn't matter nor the fallen streak at the bottom nor the slightly burned edge. All the love and kindness in the world had gone into that cake, and nothing could have made it taste better.

The ice froze deeper, crept slowly toward the swift current. Children skated gracefully, perilously, close to the dangerous edge. While we reveled in their perfect rhythm, we worried too, because the ice gave so dangerously under their weight. But the children paid no heed.

John examined a pair of skates. "They're files," he exclaimed, "just plain files, sharpened, and fitted into wood!"

"I wish I could skate like that," I said, watching the bright scarves, the flashing figures.

"If you really want to, let's borrow some skates from the Swens and practice down on the slough."

Then and there began my first skating lesson. John clamped

the smaller pair on my shoes and tightened his own with the key. Holding me upright, he ventured onto the ice. I'd never before had on skates. I clung to John as he slid away from the bank. My skates scarcely touched the ice before they slipped out from under me. John hung on and balanced me again. I leaned forward too far and again the skates sent me tumbling.

"Here," John directed, "slide like this." He left me and went skating off. Instantly the skates shot out from under me and I hit the ice with such a terrific bang that stars twinkled momentarily. I tried to get up but the skates tangled my feet and skidded in every direction.

John pulled me up. "Your ankles are weak, but they'll strengthen with practice."

I rubbed my cold hands together. Some of the enthusiasm had ebbed, and my rear still felt the thud on the ice. "Do you really think so?"

"You didn't expect to start right out and skate, did you?" He rested my body against his to prevent my skates from dashing out in dizzying circles. "Come on, let's try again. In a few days we'll be ready to join the others."

His tone was encouraging. I tried again.

I shook my head at last. "I just can't take another spill," I said. I massaged the seat of my hiking pants.

"Just once more," John begged. "You'll make it this time."

I got up on my wobbly ankles and clutched John. "Try it alone," he suggested. I tried to move away. One foot miraculously kept on sliding on a balanced keel, and as it did I cautiously raised the other, putting it forward fearfully. I'd taken my first step.

John said, "That's enough for today." But I begged for another chance, to prove it wasn't an accident.

I sat down on the snow while he unfastened the skates. My nose was so cold it ached with my breathing, and the evening chill had crept through our bodies. But all the way home I vowed I'd practice until I could skate.

One morning we woke to find the river frozen solid. Awed by it, we stood looking over the silenced river, feeling the majesty and the mightiness of Alaska's winter. For days we had watched great drifts of pancake ice moving steadily, crunching, swirling and jabbing their way toward Golovin Bay. And now the turbulent river slept. Day after day its great quilt deepened, its roar softened, until at last its length became the winter trail. Once more a life line connected the village of Blue Ridge and the Outside.

The chill air swept through our coats and sweaters. Our high-top boots stiffened. "I hope Tina finishes our parkas and mukluks soon," John said. "This cold pierces to the bone." The sun, brilliant in the snow, gave no heat; clear skies meant colder weather to come. "The dog teams will be able to cross the river in a few days," John said. "The villagers are in a hurry to get to the reindeer herd and butcher for the winter. Can't say that I blame them. Staring at one of those boiled fish heads— eyes intact—day after day would hasten my departure too!"

When, a week later, we rang the school bell only a few children answered its call. "They go to reindeer camp," the little ones told us. "Nobody come to school."

We locked the empty school and went down to the village. Was there a chance we could go along on the reindeer hunt? There was. So we went home and hunted the warmest things we could find. We wore extra underwear and socks. We put on mittens and gloves, scarves and caps. It was deeply, bitterly cold. Great excitement raged in the village. Dogs howled and yapped at their chains. Children chattered and giggled. Men straightened towlines and harnesses for the dogs. They tethered sleds to posts to keep the dogs from running away with the sleds. And when all was in readiness, they harnessed the lead dog and put the other dogs in their places along the towline.

Peter motioned to me to get on the sled, and John got on another. Each stood at the back of his sled, stepping down hard on the brake so the teeth would bite deep into the snow, and untied the rope holding the sled. The lead dog, his muscles straining at the line, felt the easing of the rope and instantly leaped forward, the team rushing behind him. Like a streak we were off, plunging down the slope of the riverbank and out onto the ice. I struggled for breath.

As soon as we hit the smooth river ice the dogs slipped and slithered, and the sleds skidded after them. The icy wind cut into my face; my coat and sweaters were no match for the bitter teeth of the day. My high-top shoes were no better. But the thrill of the swift ride, the sight of the dog teams strung out ahead and the shouting of the men kept me from noticing how really cold it was. We reached the other side of the river and climbed the bank. Here was snow again, and the dogs pulled strenuously at the sleds; to ease the load the men mushed behind. I was aware of the frozen stiffness of my shoes, the numbness of my hands and the awful cold of the winter sun. My nose ached with breathing, and white puffs of breath hung in the air.

Jumping off his sled, John came to me, his eyes watering with the cold wind. "We've got to have heat somehow," he said. We looked at the parka-clad figures around us and realized the mistake of our innocent unpreparedness. "If we ever thaw out after this day, we'll know better another time!" He found some small sticks and built a fire; we were both blue with cold. I began to shiver and my teeth chattered in a stubborn, frightening way. I thumped my fists together, and rubbed them and tried to smile at John's anxiety. I tried to move around to hide my growing chilliness, but the cold bit deeper in the piercing air. John kept fanning the tiny flame.

On numb feet I hobbled over to the tiny flame and bent to hold my swelling hands over the fire, only to draw them back with the agony of warming them too soon. Slow tears spilled out of my eyes as John rubbed my hands. The tears were of cold and pain.

"We'll never do a trick like this again," repeated John. "Maybe it's a lesson well learned."

Slowly the parka loaned to me and the fire warmed my body. A reindeer skin from the sled was wrapped around my feet, and I sat huddled and miserable—more miserable than I'd been in my life.

John came over, rubbing his face and his hands. "The men are here with the meat."

Turning, I watched them hauling the reindeer carcasses. I touched John's cold face and brushed his frozen breath from his coat collar. "It won't be long now," I chattered.

As the men rested, they cracked open the animal's leg bones, sucking and munching the marrow. "They've already bled the deer," John explained. "They'll keep the blood for later delicacies—even for ice cream."

Now that the hunt was over they were in no hurry; they laughed and joked, for this was a great day. "Why should they hurry?" John said. "The day, and the days to come, are just more hours before them. No boats to catch, no trains or busses to ride, no schedules to keep. Not even business to fret about!" Shivering, we watched them gnaw at the joints.

Huddled in fur on the homeward trip, I felt the enormity of our isolation, the starkness of the villagers' lives and the frugality with which they lived. As the sleds creaked on the trail, as the dogs strained under the whips, the thought came again: what incentive kept these people—so like us and yet so different—struggling on? Watching them alternately mush and ride and yell happily at their teams, I couldn't find it. Perhaps they didn't need one; perhaps they never grew up but only grew old in their fun-loving, gay and carefree way. Perhaps we had no more than they? They brought in meat when they were hungry, they gathered wood when the fire was low. When they needed more food they brought in furs for barter or cut wood. Yet, listening to their laughter, their good humor, we knew they had captured something of the meaning of life, something important, that often died with the coming of ambition, something that survived in the barren wastes and in these primitive outposts of another civilization. And we knew, too, that upon our return to the States this simple, unhurried, unworried way of life would be lost to us. I huddled deeper and watched the joy of their sledding. That's why some of the white men have stayed, I thought. This ability to be content with little. It might explain the presence of the squaw men—that and the fact they grew shy and wary of the outside world.

We welcomed the warmth of our house, yet were thankful for the parka, the reindeer skin and the flame out on the tundra. "We'll get tough fast this way," John declared, sipping hot coffee. "That is, if we live long enough."

"We came here to help them, and here they're helping us," I reminded him.

"That we did," John said. "Perhaps their way of life isn't as placid as it looks."

We had reason to ponder it when, days later, we opened the door to an urgent knock and stared into the face of a white man.

John brought him out of the storm and while I poured him coffee he told us he was from Council.

John looked up quickly. "Council? You mean you live at Council, where all the gold miners stopped?"

The stranger—he at once said we were to call him Tom—nodded his shaggy head, stretched out in the warmth. His lean face was weathered deep, his eyes sank sharply above the cheekbones. When he spoke his teeth showed dark and stained—a part of the price, we guessed, a white man pays to survive in a land of such simplicity.

"That's right," he said. "But what's left is mostly us old-timers—useless and forgotten. Council once was bustin' its britches. Now there's only three or four families." He leaned toward the fire and tapped his pipe on top of the stove. "You figurin' to go up there sometime? You oughtta, before you leave."

"We want to go in the spring if we can. So much depends on the months ahead."

After supper Tom stood up to go; his parka looked as gaunt as his body. "My wife's sick abed," he said. "She's going to have a baby." He hesitated, looking down at the glowing stove. Then, "You got any wood to chop? Or could I shovel snow? I gotta have some bread for my wife. We've both been sick. . . ." The pallor of illness was on his face.

I wrapped two loaves of bread and tucked in a can of soup and several cans of milk and a little cheese. "You're very welcome to it," John said. "Let us know when we can help and how everything goes for both of you."

Tom turned to me. "When you come to Council, we'll be

there. Me and my wife have the keys to the biggest hotel. You can bet we'll do our best to show you around."

The cold met him at the door; snow swirled at his stooped shoulders. In a moment he had joined the night and the storm. John came back to the fire. A great excitement kindled in his face as he leaned to kiss me. "Dolly," he said, "don't let's allow a thing in this world to stop us from making the trip to Council. It'll be something we'll never forget." I shared his eagerness and I hoped nothing would prevent our going in the spring.

Chapter 5

Our life settled into routine. The mail came by dogsled, turning the day of its arrival into a veritable holiday. Every chore was dropped as we gathered up the precious letters, the first in many weeks—and the last for at least a month. We took turns reading, opening each letter in order of its postmark so that the news reached us as it had happened, for our families had written every week even though the mail was delivered all at once.

As we opened the bulging envelopes, we faltered at the first endearments, our voices trailing off. At the final good-bys, we sat folding and unfolding the pages, our eyes brimming unashamed. Not now, but tomorrow, we'd face forward once more.

The long winter nights came early; the little red house became even more of a refuge, for without a dog team we were glad to huddle near the roaring stove while howling winds shook the foundations. The wizened organ often rang with a nasal, off-tune cadence as we sang. When our voices grew hoarse, we turned to the Edison phonograph we'd lugged from the States. Its cylindrical records, worn and warped, screeched and wobbled under the dull needle. But no matter! The music fired us with enthusiasm and gaiety, often sweeping us into a round of hilarious dancing that left us gasping for breath.

"The neighbors probably think we've gone crazy," John said.

"I suppose we ought to call on them more often. But after a day at the school, I don't want to do anything but relax!"

The hours left after cooking and cleaning gave little time for laundry—boiling it, struggling to get it dry, ironing. The backbreaking job never ended; it was waiting when I finished the bread, cake and cooky baking and the housecleaning. Now and then we waved at our neighbors or called to them from the path, or met them in the village, but we had very little idea of what was going on.

Now I paced the floor, suddenly remembering yesterday, when Mrs. Swen had stepped from the path until Mrs. Rance had gone by. And the day before, when Mr. Rance left Mr. Swen in obviously bad temper.

I turned to John. "Is it foolish of me, or have you noticed a change in the way they behave toward each other?"

He shrugged. "It's just the silence and the lack of familiar faces coming and going."

I agreed; Mr. Rance's face could look bad-tempered at a distance; Mrs. Swen probably had a perfectly good reason for waiting down on the path. Yet, when I was lying in the darkness, a premonition of the outbreak of civil war returned.

Fears seemed nonsense in the morning on the trek to the schoolhouse. We admired our students, glad for their cheerful smiles.

"I wish we had a library for the bright and eager ones," John said. "I guess we'll have to make our own books."

Evening chores took longer now. Beneath the ice the river lowered, thereby making the job of water lifting more dangerous. Each time, as the ice hole was reopened, John leaned deeper to bring the bucket to the surface. Roaring fires that never went out must be fed; still, each morning, the nailheads on the walls were frosty, ice froze on the water buckets and thickened on the windowpanes.

By November Tina had our parkas and mukluks ready. Trying on the parkas for the first time left us gasping as we poked our heads through the neckholes into the hoods. Tina smiled and pointed at the delicate design she'd made at the bottom and on the sleeves and hood. "This fur," she explained, pointing at the edges of the hood, "he is wolverine. He keep your breath from freezing with these long hairs." She pulled the dried hay from inside the mukluks. "This hay keep your feet warm and dry, you see?" We fingered the soft reindeer hair, admired the stitching. "You wind this strap around your ankle and tie in front to keep mukluk tight. This drawstring at top, he keep cold and snow out."

We looked at ourselves in the mirror. Suddenly the odor that had belonged to the villagers became our own. Heat and wear and the closeness of human bodies made it stronger.

November brought thoughts of Thanksgiving. Even though there would be no turkey dinner nor family gathering, we made plans, for it would be our first such holiday together.

"We can have ptarmigan," said John, "or fish or rabbit!"

"Or leg of reindeer." I grimaced a bit at the thought.

We made it ptarmigan, caught in one of John's snares across the river, and pumpkin pie. We filled in the menu with salad, peas and rolls. We prepared the dinner together in the kitchen, with its warmth and fragrance of freshly baked bread and rolls, while outside the snow came down in swirls and settled anew over paths, trails and rooftops. No one stirred in the little village. Dogs huddled down in their holes and buried their noses in fur. Men shoved more wood into potbellied stoves. Children stayed close to the fireside. It was a day to shut out the storm and snuggle deeper; to sit close to each other; to lift feet from the chill of the floor to the warmth of the roaring fire. It was a day to sit in the darkening shadows and listen for the call of a great Voice in the silence that embraced us.

We found two candles that the Swens or some other occupant of the house had left behind. With these and the figures of the Pilgrim Fathers the children had made out of clothespins we set our table as well as we could. And when we sat down to eat, John asked the blessing as though we were sitting down to crystal and sterling. Neither of us missed the linen or china, for we had the spirit of the day. Later in the evening our neighbors called. We put more wood in the range, popped corn and gathered around the miniature organ. When the evening ended, Miss Charles, the Swens and Mr. and Mrs. Rance pulled on parkas and waded back into the night.

John closed the door with a puzzled frown. "No use denying it—I can feel something," he said, "something that's not quite as it was."

"It's like a fire smoldering. Nothing seemed to break through. But Mr. Rance's eyes looked bleak."

"I can't put my finger on it. I don't know whether we've done something, or if it's the fault of someone else."

We tried to analyze it. But there was no answer. We'd worked hard and long, trying to do our share. Yet the feeling of trouble hovered over us, dimming our evening and leaving us anxious and worried.

The passing days confirmed snatches of rumor. Mrs. Swen first hinted of trouble when she ran down for a cup of coffee

on the following Saturday. It was a disagreement over the orphanage plans. A few hours later Mrs. Rance ran over with a
loaf of bread, and she mentioned the disagreement from her
point of view. Miss Charles, who felt everyone owed her respect
and homage, was next. But her troubles were different. She
frightened me a little with her coal-black eyes, her protruding
chin, her pouter pigeon breast.

"Why on earth," she demanded, "haven't you folks been to
call on me?" She stared down at me. "If you weren't newlyweds, I'd consider you deliberately rude."

I felt wicked. I felt very wicked; I felt as if I'd committed
an unpardonable sin. I could only stare at her double chin and
heavy face without saying a word, as a flush mounted to the
roots of my hair. We'd not meant to ignore her or be unkind.
But as newlyweds we clung together, enjoying every hour, enjoying the isolation all the more among these older and more
experienced people.

As the weeks passed, instead of joining the others we kept to
the house even more. The snows were deeper and the cold never
eased. Without a team, without snowshoes, there was no place
to go except through the village or down on the river trail.

"You shouldn't be on the trail," Mr. Rance warned us. "The
dog teams are dangerous. And if a team met you on the trail,
they might jump you before the driver could stop them." He
told us tales of white men who had lost their lives, of children
savagely mauled. "That's the reason you rarely see the team
dogs loose. It's a dangerous thing up here."

Before, we had pitied the dogs tied to their stakes. Now we
remembered how the native dogs strained and tugged at their
stakes as we passed. We never indulged in this pity again.

Now and then we trudged to the river where the village

women squatted to fish through the ice. Tina often handed her string to me. "See," Tina said, "you must bob it up and down and then jerk. Big fish will see hook. Then he grab quick."

So I let the string drop through the hole into the river. I pulled and jerked the string rhythmically as she had shown me, and then something grabbed the hook *quick,* and with an excited scream, I pulled hard.

"Ah-ha!" Tina said, and all the women laughed in glee at the sleek grayling on the ivory hook. Tina reached over and pulled the hook from the fish's mouth. While the fish lay freezing, John examined the hook.

"A bent nail fastened in a piece of ivory. I'll bet Ivory Pete will make one of these for me."

I had been kneeling on a bag of grass; I got up, straightening my cold legs. With John I went back to the little village, rubbing my cheeks and nose. "I'll never make a successful native," I said. "The cold soaks right through every hair in this parka."

John put his arm through mine. His lips were as blue as mine. "We'll get used to it," he said.

"How? I wear long woolies from top to bottom and itch twenty-four hours a day. I put on wool socks over wool socks. I button on every sweater I can filch from you and put this parka over all. I wear a wool stocking cap and over that goes my parka hood!" I caught his hands as I climbed the bank. "And still I can't keep my teeth from chattering. I think even my blood is freezing!"

"Here," John said, "we'll run up this hill and that'll warm you." So we went racing up the hill, slipping repeatedly on the glazed snow.

Mrs. Rance called to us from her door. "Watch out," she said, "the path is dangerous."

We looked at each other; the word danger greeted us at every step. If we ran down the hill, if we ran up the hill, if we took a walk beyond the paths, if we went fishing too far out on the ice—someone was sure to warn us.

Mrs. Rance continued, "We're having everyone to Christmas dinner—the Whites from Golovin too. You plan on coming."

"Can't we help with the food?"

She shook her head. "Mr. Rance is going to Nome and he'll bring a frozen turkey."

"Wow!" exclaimed John as we went home. "Figured at twice the Outside price, that turkey'll cost a pretty penny!"

Turkey! I nodded happily.

As Christmas neared, home and the Outside, with the glittering crowds and stores, the hushed, secretive atmosphere, haunted us. "Think of the tinsel—the trees—the packages."

"I hope nobody will spoil the day," John said.

Sharp words, close to our door, interrupted him. We sat rooted to our chairs, feeling like eavesdroppers but not able to move. "Whether you like it or not," the cold voice went on, "it'll be done the way I say. As builder I'm responsible for the results!"

As the voice faded, John and I breathed again. "That's what I mean," he said. "It's a battle between two determined men."

"What'll happen?"

"In the States it wouldn't seem so important. Up here neither can move without running into the other." He began to pace the floor. "If it becomes a fight to the finish, it could mean the end for all of us."

"It makes me wish for spring right now! Just having more daylight and sunshine helps the world look brighter."

But such thoughts couldn't dampen our spirits for long.

Christmas was close. There would be Hans, the old sourdough, scarred and rough from years in the wilderness. Toothless now, with a reddish beard covering his cheekbones, his hair snipped any which way, he still looked roguishly at every woman who ventured near, kidding her in the language of his youth. Everyone liked him and no one took offense at his ancient quips.

Then there would be the owner of the lighter and his wife, remnants of the Gold Rush, too; and the squaw men from the restaurant; and Old John, the trader, and his wife.

We rushed plans for the Christmas program at the school, creating and directing plays, tableaux, recitations and songs. Sheets and toweling were used for angels' robes, more sheets were hung for the stage curtains; wire was strung across the front of the room for the other decorations. Colored paper chains swung from window to window, pictures depicting the coming of Christ were drawn on the blackboards. The excitement caught us all in a web of eagerness.

When finally the afternoon arrived, scrubbed and beaming children entered with mothers, fathers and aged grandparents. They came silently in padded mukluks and sat enchanted with the colored paper chains, the singing angels and the Christmas music and tableaux. After it was over, they stood patiently waiting to shake our hands and to give us the presents they'd kept hidden under their parkas.

At last we stepped out into the shadows that lay deep on the river of ice and snow. Down in the village someone was tossing fish to the howling dogs. Soon a great moon would rise and the snow would sparkle in the cold and the Northern Lights would crackle as they pushed deeply into the sky. But for us, in this hour, we could only stand alone in the blue twilight as evening settled and then climb wearily and thankfully to the weathered door of our house.

Inside, we spread the gifts from the village—ivory napkin holders, penholders, bracelets, and ivory faces of grinning bears tinted with herbs and berries, a miniature kayak complete with paddles, and a spear to be used for seal hunting. And an ivory fishhook.

"If tomorrow is as peaceful . . ." John said.

On Christmas Day new snow had fallen. We looked out on a land of whiteness and drifts piled many feet high at the windows. We jumped out of bed and ran to the warmth of the stove.

"Merry Christmas," called John, poking the fire.

Watching him that Christmas morning, I realized that the faith upon which we had built our marriage was in his every movement, that the courage we needed was there, that integrity lay in his eyes, that his sympathy gave me riches. I went to him and put my arms around him. "Merry Christmas, darling," I said. "A very merry Christmas."

He put the lid of the stove over the flames, then hugged me to him. We stood silent a moment, close to each other.

"As long as we never take each other for granted . . ."

The wind rattled the windows, whistled at the house and sent a spray of snow into the air. Breakfasting hastily, we turned to cleaning and dusting. While I finished the last dish John went to the river for water. We filled the folding rubber tub with water heated on the stove and both used the same water before emptying the tub. At first this bit of extemporizing bothered us, but not after John had carried so many loads of water from the river below.

"It's not exactly according to Hoyle," John said, "but who cares about Hoyle? You take your bath first, and I'll take the second shift."

"Next time," I said, "you'll be first!"

I had just finished dressing when we heard the dogs yapping in frenzy. Running to the window, we saw a dog team far down the trail. Down in the village bedlam reigned. Nowhere else could the appearance of another human being bring such a welcome. Now we understood the lonely people we'd met at every village outpost.

Suddenly another shout went up from the village. "Another team!" John yelled excitedly as we put on parkas and joined the crowd lining the riverbanks.

In a crescendo of noise the first sled stopped. "Mr. Carr and his wife," John said, "and in the second sled Old John, the trader, and his wife."

It was a day we would not easily forget, this day with the sourdoughs. Their clothing was clean and old and faded. I wondered when Old John had last worn a tie and then I grinned at the thought of a tie around that lined and scarred neck.

Then Sam, the café owner, spoke to me. He remembered my first taste of his reindeer steak at Golovin. "You like it now?" he asked in a toothless grin.

Mrs. Carr sat beside me just before dinner. "Are you planning on staying in Alaska long?" she asked. She was a gray-haired lady, perhaps fifty.

"No," I said, "not more than a year."

She patted my knee. "It's lonely at first. But after a while it doesn't matter. If you stay much longer than a year, you won't be happy Outside."

At the table Mr. Carr squared the linen dinner napkin under

his chin, launching into the turkey with the appetite of a man just off the trail. Finally he came up for air and wrinkled his brow at me. "First turkey I've et in years. Forgot how good it was. Been eatin' duck and goose and ptarmigan too long and forgettin' the farmyard!" He chewed some more. "Guess you haven't et wild things very much, huh? You like the gamy taste?"

"Not much," I told him honestly, "but I didn't like canned milk or dried eggs either. And now I'm used to both."

He wiped gravy from his chin. "If you stay long enough you'll turn into a sourdough." Then he spoke to Mr. Rance. "That's right, ain't it? Say, how's that big elephant coming along—that orphanage?"

Only the rattle of a fork and a spoon could be heard. Tongues were tied to every roof. Then Mr. Rance and Mr. Swen found theirs.

"Elephant!" Mr. Rance's thin face sharpened.

"I've been telling them it's wrong. Why, those rooms absolutely——" Mr. Swen stopped, anger choking him.

Miss Charles broke in. "What we need is a hospital, not an orphanage!"

Mr. Carr's innocent question left a ghastly trail of silence and embarrassment.

Mrs. Rance urged all to eat more turkey, more dressing, more pumpkin pie. She passed candy and nuts and fruit cake.

John turned the conversation to Old John, the trader. "Weren't you here during the Gold Rush at Council?"

Old John nodded his bristly head. "Sure was. Mined up there for years." He threw his hands in a vast circle. "Out on the river it sure was a sight! People, boats, barges swarming everywhere! Everybody trying to beat the next guy!"

"How did a town grow up there?"

Old John sucked at his pipe. "By this here very river! Every foot of lumber, every pot and pan went right past this very window! Far as I know, it's all still there!" He relaxed with the satisfaction of having important information to offer.

Mrs. Rance turned to me, laughing her thin laugh, "Don't let Old John talk you into going! It isn't nearly as rosy as it sounds."

Mr. Rance joined in the warning. "Nowadays it just isn't a trip for a woman."

I looked at John. He wasn't listening to Mr. Rance. He was seeing the Gold Rush as Old John described it, living its excitement. All evening he questioned the sourdoughs, and when we rose to leave he was ready to go up the river, over the winter trails.

"Wake up, John," I said, pushing open our door, "this is only Christmas!"

"But we've got to go this spring! Why, we'd never forgive ourselves if we passed up the chance."

"But John, what if——" I slipped out of my parka, hesitating now as he turned toward me.

"What do you mean, what if?"

I couldn't look into his eager eyes. I drank from the bucket of water and came back to sit on the couch. "John," I said, feeling the weight of what I must tell him, "I think I'm—I think we're going to have a baby."

Instantly he was kneeling beside me, holding me close to his chest. And we sat there, trying to look into this new future.

"That changes everything," John said. He pulled me up and pushed back my hair.

"We'll still go to Council," I said. "After all, I'll only be six months along."

"That may be," he said, "but right now you're going to bed."

Neither of us slept well that night. The baby's coming created a whole new batch of problems. Where would the child be born? Would we go Outside? How could I teach after the birth—a requisite if we were to stay here? And a doctor . . . Already, too, we'd spoken about asking for a transfer next year to a village of our own somewhere on the Yukon. And if we did go to the Yukon, how could we raise a baby without benefit of doctor, nurse or hospital? Not even my mother would be here to bolster my morale.

John felt my wakefulness. "Do you suppose there's a medical book we could borrow?"

I thought of Miss Charles. I could ask her. But when the thought came the next day I postponed my many questions. This was our secret, and for a time we'd keep it our own.

Chapter 6

SHORTLY AFTER CHRISTMAS, when school re-opened, I learned that the secret of pregnancy couldn't be kept. Each morning as I pushed open the schoolhouse door, I leaned dizzily against the wall, fighting off a curtain of darkness. Throughout the days it became a race between that curtain and a gulp of icy air at the door or the reviving touch of John's strong hand. Afterward I came back to my desk, listening to the little ones read though my head throbbed and I seemed always hungry. Once the blackness was swifter than John. When I awoke in his arms, frightened faces surrounded me. "Help me up," I pleaded, ashamed that I had fainted.

"Take it easy," he said. "You're not going to stay here. You're going home!"

"No," I said, struggling up. "I'll be all right now."

The children continued their work silently though each one must have known what the trouble was.

At the end of the day John and I went home, fixed dinner, did the remaining housework and rested. It was February now, and the increased rivalry and bitterness among our neighbors made a complete break seem inevitable. We'd planned a St. Valentine's Day party, and worried now about its outcome.

"Our first party," I said, "and it has to be with bickering friends. If only they'd relax and have fun!"

"Maybe if we just keep on ignoring their differences, they'll try, too, for this one evening."

On the final afternoon I called John in for his haircut. I wrapped an old cloth around his neck to catch the clippings. I asked, "Anything new in the air?"

He grimaced as the clippers ran close to his ears. "They're the only ears I've got!" he yelped. "Just now on the trail," he said, "Rance and Swen were quarreling. Hey, for Pete's sake, leave a few of those hairs, will you?"

I picked up the comb and scissors. Tiny bits of hair flew into my face, lodged in my mouth and covered my hands. "You know—" I angled my body into a question mark in order to see a little better—"putting a bowl on your head might be a good idea. I'll be scratching for hours to come."

"It's no better for me, but if you want a bowl haircut, why I——"

"No, no," I said hastily.

"No use fretting. Either we cut or we let it grow—and I'm not ready to let it grow. By the time we get back to the States you'll be so good at this, you'll never want to give up fifty cents to a barber!"

I combed his top hair between my middle finger and forefinger, and clipped off the uneven edges. Somewhere I'd seen that done and it worked beautifully.

As soon as I'd finished John's haircut, he took off the cloth and wrapped it around my neck.

"Wait," I said, "I'll get the mirror." Originally my hair had been shingled at the back, with a slight front bang.

"How short?" John asked, opening and closing the scissors.

I looked in the mirror. "To the bottom of my ears."

First he tackled the left side, cutting around to the middle of the back. Then he switched to the right side. Arriving at the back, he found the cuts didn't quite coincide. He cut a bit more from the left side, which instantly became shorter than the right. I began to get nervous.

"You're past my ear lobes."

He began to cut the bangs. "Say where!" He pointed the scissor blades at my forehead.

"Go slow," I said, "and then I'll have some left when you're through."

He handed me the scissors and took the mirror. "Do it yourself. I'll never manage." The hair still zigged and zagged.

"Thank heavens, hair does grow again." John looked at his haircut critically.

I got the broom and dustpan. "At least we won't have to bother for another two weeks."

At six-thirty we bathed close to the range. "It's your turn to be first," I insisted. But he waited until I was done before claiming the tub. He lowered himself into ten inches of water and soaped his hairy arms.

"I can understand why a sourdough may go from spring to spring without a bath. In fact, a man could go native up here without a woman to urge him on."

"You mean you'd let your hair and whiskers grow like Jack, the squaw man?"

"After all," John said as he emptied the tub, "if no one cares about your dirty face, why clean it?"

With the first knock, John opened the door to Miss Charles. Briefly John glanced at me, remembering the evening the nurse had knocked and we'd called, "Come in." When no one entered, John had opened the door to find Miss Charles glaring from the threshold. "Don't you know," she burst out, "that you should open the door for visitors?" We apologized, realizing finally that for Miss Charles no one ever apologized enough. Perhaps she was too old to be alone in Alaska. Perhaps life had dealt bitterly with her. At any rate, we now felt uncomfortable when she was near.

Tonight her dark silk party dress emphasized the whiteness of her hair. While I helped her take off her parka, John welcomed the superintendent and his wife. Seconds later the Swens arrived.

Little quakes began in the pit of my stomach. Would everyone bury the hatchet this evening? Or would they hack and chop to the end?

I seated them carefully—the women not too close, the men with John between them. The quaking in my stomach wouldn't stop. I brought in coffee immediately and the tension gradually lessened. I began to breathe easier, my mind taking in the details of refilling cups, of passing sugar and cream.

John asked Mr. Rance about his dog team—only Mr. Rance owned dogs so there could be no competitive boasting—and Mr. Rance rose eagerly to the bait. And when I asked Miss Charles about the illness of the tubercular woman, she told us how she had died.

"To think," she said bitterly, "a mother without a minute to herself, slowly dying, right before the eyes of her children."

"But to live like that," spoke up Mrs. Swen, "with all the members of the family eating from the same dish, drinking from the same cup . . ."

"Something should be done, but I don't know what." Miss Charles looked balefully at Mrs. Rance. "Isn't there a thing the Bureau can do for such cases?"

Mrs. Rance's mouth tightened defensively. "If there is, they haven't told us."

I rose hurriedly. In a minute they'd be quarreling. Now was the time to suggest some game. And much to my amusement they all seemed relieved to have a chance to try Musical Chairs.

While I played the music, John kept the game going, removing a chair at the end of each round. When only two contestants were left and a single chair, John called the game a tie. I brought more coffee, the Jello, the cake.

Suddenly Miss Charles turned to Mr. Rance. "Is that orphange finished now?" At the word "orphanage" I cringed as if someone had struck me.

"It should be!" Mr. Rance said. His face flushed. Everyone bent to his coffee.

Mr. Swen was slowly turning purple. John scraped back his chair, saying amiably, "I still don't see how that building went up so fast, here in the wilderness! It beats me how you ever got so much work done."

Mr. Swen relaxed. Everyone smiled with relief and drank more coffee. Shortly after, they left.

When John closed the door on the last parka, we sank exhausted to the couch. "Whew!" he whistled softly, "I haven't an unfrayed nerve left in my body."

I rubbed my forehead. "And to think this is only February! What will the feud be like by spring?"

John stretched on the couch. "If we consider staying longer than a year, we must ask for a transfer to our own village."

The question had come up before but never so urgently. "Right now I'd like to leave at once." I pressed my temples. "What about the baby's birth? Will it be up here?"

He took my hand and held it close. "It's late and we can't settle that tonight. Come to bed."

Lying in the darkness, I knew we must soon make a decision. In the quietness now, all the arguments came again. The baby was probably due in the middle of August. Following the ice break-up in May, we could go Outside to stay; or I might go alone, arriving in Seattle sometime in July. To John would be left the job of moving wherever the Bureau transferred us, while, down in the States, the birth would barely be over before I would have to sail again for a strange new place, arriving in the chill of fall.

I understood that John wanted to stay another year; I felt it in his words as he spoke of building a financial reserve by investing in a lumber mill. If we both stayed in Alaska, the baby might arrive unattended—might, indeed, coincide with our transfer. Then too, supplies must be ordered quickly so that they would arrive on the first boat. Tomorrow I must borrow the Rances' catalogue.

I rose and drank a glass of water, and the icy chill of the floor was sharp on my bare feet. Its shock cleared my head. Suddenly the decision was made. I would stay with John. Together we'd travel to the new station. I crept shivering into bed. How could I have doubted it? I rolled over and put my arm across John. And after that I slept.

The days lengthened. Even though winter lay heavily on the river and across the tundra, we felt the mood of another season. When the darkness of snow-filled skies passed, the sun stayed a few minutes longer on the children's desks and out on the hill where the children tried their barrel-stave skis.

On one of March's warmer days we attended the Eskimo church. In the small, unventilated room we sat and listened

among the old, the crippled, the sick. Our friend Ali preached
in a mixture of English and the local dialect. The songbooks
had come from somewhere—no one seemed to know how.

Ali tapped me on the shoulder. "Will you play for us?" he
asked.

Some of the organ keys were broken and made no sound, but
it didn't matter. After the first few chords of "Rock of Ages"
the eager voices of the congregation drowned out the chugging
organ. More songs and an earnest prayer ended the service.

The villagers clasped our hands as we went out into the
fresh air. "I've gone to church all my life," John said, "but
never have I seen people more attentive. Did you see their
faces?"

I nodded. I wondered if, up here, alone, without the distrac-
tion of what we called civilization, God seemed closer.

We watched the bobbing heads going down the hill—the
toothless ones, the tubercular and the dying. John shook his
head. "You and I have so much to be thankful for."

We turned homeward. The breeze of new life lifted the low
branches and deep inside me life's movements echoed it like the
soft pulse of a bird.

April was gentle, on the breath of the new season. The melting snow turned old and brown. The stirring river rose over
its clinging ice and froze again at night. Inexorably the river's
quickening pressure buckled the surface on which we had
walked.

Looking out onto this season that held so much we could not
anticipate, John said, "At home everyone is getting ready for
Easter and church."

"With new clothes and spring hats." And daffodils blooming.

And trillium in the woods. I couldn't see the melting ice on the trail for the mist in my eyes. But when John raised my chin, there were no tears.

The fragrance of morning coffee came from the kitchen. "What'll it be?" I asked. "Dried eggs scrambled or dried eggs scrambled?"

John pondered the matter. "Oh, well, you might try scrambling them for a change. I noticed some bacon in the storeroom. Let's don't save it any longer." He came back with canned pineapple, apple butter and tomato juice.

"That's all of the pineapple and tomato juice. Should we have them both?" I said.

"At Easter, without new clothes, spring hats and hams, this will be our great indulgence of the day!"

"Then sit down and ask the blessing, and pray that what remains will last."

Entering the church later, we nodded to those around us. I saw Mrs. Rance's thin lips tighten as Mrs. Swen leaned toward me; farther over, Mr. Swen's jaw was tense. Mr. Rance nodded once. The services began. Above the organ the songs rang out, often in words we couldn't understand. We glanced at the rapt faces of the villagers. There were no spring hats atop the greasy braids of hair; no colorful suits and dresses amid the winter parkas; no purses dangling from those weathered, ungloved hands; no pumps to take the place of grass-lined mukluks. But our preacher was giving his people what all preachers hope to give—hope and faith in God. His people hadn't come to him with new hats and empty hearts. They had come because they had need of his message and belief.

When we rose and milled toward the door, we knew this was an Easter we'd remember. It wasn't spring or trilliums or jonquils, or new hats. It was the Resurrection. We pushed toward the door, not wanting to be reminded of the quarrels of our neighbors.

We went back up the trail toward home. Ali called to us and we waited at the doorstep. We made coffee and heated the hot cross buns I'd prepared.

As Ali ate hungrily, I thought of his hut in the village; his buxom wife; the six children eating, sleeping, in one small room. We'd seen the deerskin beds; the kettle of fish in the middle of the floor; Ali, the scholar, trying to grasp the meaning of fractions; and today we'd seen Ali the Preacher, vibrant, persuasive . . .

With more coffee, he relaxed. "I came during the Gold Rush with two other men," he explained. "We found lots of gold— but others stole our claim."

"Couldn't you stop them?" John asked.

"You've never seen men hungry for gold, have you? So hungry they'll kill and steal and lie. Our claim turned out to be one of the richest. But not for us."

"And after that you stayed——"

Ali nodded. The fire cracked in the big stove. The breeze outside stiffened against the house. "Yes," he said, "I stayed." He emptied the cup of coffee. "But lots of men left their babies——"

The dogs were howling and yelping in the village. Ali nodded toward the river. "Someone is trying to train a deer to pull his sled." We heard shouting. "The deer's afraid of the dogs. He will be dangerous."

"What will happen?" I asked.

"Maybe the driver will get back, maybe not. Maybe sometime his body will be found on the tundra."

After Ali left, we went back to the warm fire. "Do you really think he'll make it?" I asked John. The thought of the sled driver's mangled body frozen on the tundra haunted me. There were wolves, and I feared to think of what wolves would do to a man's body.

"Look," said John, "this is Easter. There isn't a thing we can do for the driver. But there's a family down in the village that's starving. The father is so ill with tuberculosis he can't get out of bed. Ali said the three children are starving."

"And no one trying to help them?"

"At this time of year, even the Eskimos are short of fish and other food. I thought maybe——"

We went to the storeroom. Our supplies were getting pitifully low. "I'll make some soup for them, and we'll take some bread."

"Can we spare any rice or milk?" He looked at the nearly empty shelves.

Down in the village Ali joined us. "Here is where they live."

Inside, the little children sat quietly, too weak to play. A baby cried piteously. Lying on a bed of skins, the father pleaded with cavernous eyes. He raised himself to speak, but the effort seemed too great and he lay back, covering his face.

Dusk was falling. Blue haze drifted and settled slowly on the horizon. The sun had left, and the night-cold was coming, freezing the water that crept to the top of the ice on the river. Our breath was condensing as we trudged home. The warmth of the house greeted us, but our hearts felt a far greater warmth. John pushed wood into a yawning stove and then sat before it. I felt the pulsebeat of our own baby. That hungry baby could have been ours, the scrawny legs, the distended stomach. John rocked and was silent.

"You know," I said, "perhaps, after all, we should write the folks about our baby. If anything happened——" But even as I spoke I knew neither of us would add this burden to their anxieties.

Chapter 7

AFTER EASTER we shed the winter woolens at last. The change was like a tonic. I suddenly felt pounds lighter and very frisky and gay, although the weight of pregnancy was on me. Before my own pregnancy I had paid no attention to the swelling bodies of others. Now, abruptly, my own appalled me. Without maternity dresses to disguise my condition, I was glad of the fullness of the parka. A cotton house dress hugged me tightly in the wrong places and my skirts gaped open at the waist. Stockings no longer met the garter belt and slips bulged alarmingly. Even so I felt better. Reaching far back in the closet, I brought out long-unused oxfords. After rolling black cotton stockings just above the knee and tying my shoes, I looked down at myself, feeling chilled without the straw-padded mukluks and the clinging underwear.

John came to the door and whistled sharply. Ignoring the whistle, I finished dressing. "Like the other animals, I'm shedding. And I feel spry as a kitten until I look in the miror!" I turned for a profile. "See what I mean?"

He couldn't keep his face straight, and even though I knew how I looked, I suddenly resented his merriment. "Laugh if you want to," I said scathingly. "If I had some decent clothes——" I began combing my hair briskly. I'd never pitied myself before, but now a picture of the cast-off garter belt, the puckered slip, the gaping placket, the rolled stockings, rushed over me, and in abject misery tears welled to my eyes.

"Dolly!" John started to comfort me, but I glared at him through my tears. I didn't want his pity; I didn't want my own either. I just wanted to be left alone until I'd had my cry, and then everything would be all right again. As if he understood, he turned and began rummaging in the desk. "Are you going to send an order for the baby's things?"

That cleared the air. I wiped away the tears and brought the pen. We went to the kitchen table. "Just think! He'll be the first grandchild. Mother and Dad will be thrilled!"

John opened the Sears catalogue to the page headed *layettes*. We stared bewildered at all the little shirts, diapers, dresses, nighties and slips. John was aghast. "How much will he need?"

I was as baffled. "I don't know. I've never had a baby before."

We turned to bottles, powders and safety pins. We stared at each other apprehensively. "I think you should write your mother," John said. "Why—why——" The magnitude of the task, our complete lack of knowledge of how to care for the coming baby, left him speechless.

We turned to the clothes. "Let's get a complete layette, one that isn't too skimpy or too large, and let Sears worry about the sizes, the quantity," John suggested.

"We'll still need blankets. Bottles, too."

We felt a little breathless all the rest of the week. Now for the first time the baby seemed really ours. Before he was just a tiny pulsebeat, an unknown quantity. Now, suddenly, he began to be someone we could plan for.

Mr. Swen came to the door, his face inflamed. "We're leaving! I've just resigned."

"Leaving! But this is the middle of April! And the ice isn't fit for traveling!"

Mr. Swen glowered. "I can't stand the quarrels with Rance any longer! Just now, out there on the job, he jumped me again. I'm afraid one of these days I'll lose my temper and knock him down!"

"What about the orphanage children?" I asked.

He shrugged. "The Rances think they can run it better. Well, let them!" He rose, some of the bitterness gone.

"Maybe you'll change your mind," John suggested.

But Mr. Swen said, "Not a chance. I've resigned as of the end of the month."

As the door closed, John said unhappily, "The ice will be even worse by then."

Uneasiness settled swiftly. "Did you write for our transfer?" I don't want to stay *here* another year," I said.

"Nor do I. I asked for a village on the Yukon, and we should be hearing soon." School was to close in two weeks.

We urged the children to finish their reed baskets and put the last touches on the booklets they had made.

"Each face has something of its own," I told John as we watched the children at work. We were planning for our son, and all children became important to us.

Meanwhile, tension grew. "Feels like dynamite ready to blast," John said. "Look outside. See Mr. Swen's back? Even from here he looks stubborn and explosive!"

"If only there were other friends to see!"

John nodded. "It's hard to believe that small wrongs and little words can rankle so. Why, they're like open sores."

The question of who was to board Mrs. Ames, the new matron arriving, was another black cloud on the horizon. No one felt responsible, in view of the food supplies.

"It isn't up to me," Mrs. Rance said. "It's up to the Swens."

"Why should I be expected to cook and wait on her?" Mrs. Swen said. "She's not my guest. Let the Rances feed her."

John said gravely, "Every day the tempest grows in the old teapot! I can see now how prospecting partners might begin to hate and then to murder!"

I began wiping the supper dishes. "Mrs. Swen invited us to go on a picnic tomorrow. It's Ned's birthday. I'm worried now about having accepted."

"And miss being out in the sunshine? Why, Dolly, both of us need fresh air! And besides, it may be our last time to visit with the Swens, and I enjoy them when the Rances aren't around."

I turned from the cupboard. "But, John, we can't do anything to jeopardize our job with the Bureau! And if Mr. Rance sees fit to misconstrue the invitation, why, our job, our transfer, could suffer!"

"Nonsense," said John. He helped put away the dishes. "Of course, if we don't get a transfer and have to spend another year here, it would be plenty rough if the boss was sore at us!" He whistled softly. "Wouldn't we hate that, having seen what can happen!"

The next day was bright and clear. The quietness was that of the great earth coming to life; the pussywillows had gently shaken their silken buds; the alder bushes, raising branches to the warmth, unfurled; the grass on the tundra lifted and drank from the deepening water-wells at its feet. Out on the snowless track of the hills, the ptarmigan and the rabbit would soon be turning the brown of the earth after a winter of whiteness. Overhead, the Canadian geese began to honk and wheel and the mallard ducks stretched their necks in swift, silent flight.

Yes, the great earth was waking. But the ice sprawled across the river, squeezing and smothering the restless water. Soon the ice must yield to a youthful, vigorous river. And on that day the ocean would open to the Bay, the boats would steam upriver, and the Outside would flood us with accumulated holiday mail, months old.

The picnic lunch was almost ready when John said, "Dolly, would you like to go back to the States and have our baby there?"

No more struggling against ice and snow. No more watery eggs, smelly onion flakes, slushy potatoes. Instead there would be life, throngs of people—our people, people who loved and understood us. And there would be home and safety for our baby.

"Would you like that?" asked John. I watched him bending over the picnic basket. And then I saw his face as it had been when he spoke of the gold fields at Ophir, the ghost town of Council, traveling the Yukon with his own dog team. If we left Alaska now we would never return, and all the rest of our lives we would wonder and wish—and regret.

I pushed away the picture of home. "We'd never get to Council if we left now. Let's stay another year."

John tipped my chin. "Do you really want to stay?" I felt his swift hug. "Then that's settled. Get your coat."

We met the Swens at the orphanage. Walking, climbing, we huffed a bit in the warmth of the sun. After some miles we rested and ate, letting the solitude soothe us.

"If the past months could have been like this," Mr. Swen said at last, "our plans to stay until we'd saved a little money would have come true."

"Have you been in Alaska before?" I asked.

"Seven years ago, when we were first married." There was a hint of sadness in Mrs. Swen's thin voice, and Mr. Swen stirred restlessly, crossing and uncrossing his heavy boots as she went on. "There'll never be anyone but ourselves to worry about. But the first time there was a baby, a baby that died."

For a long moment we sat stunned. A baby . . . I imagined bearing a child up here, without a doctor, a nurse, a hospital. And I could imagine the Swens' despair and helplessness and the agony of self-blame, and the hopelessness when the baby died. The baby would be buried up here somewhere, somewhere on the tundra.

"We didn't know," I said lamely. There is so much one can feel, so little one can put into words. "We'd no idea."

John gripped Mr. Swen's folded arm. Then Mrs. Swen and I gathered the remains of the picnic. "I suppose you know we're going to have a baby," I said, seeking to ease her melancholy.

She looked up and her smile came quick and warm. "We didn't know," she said. "Parkas are such good Mother Hubbards."

"Due in August," John said. "I hope he won't come early."

"He?" Mrs. Swen smiled. "You men always expect a boy!"

The sun was sinking; the evening brought chilliness. We kept up a good pace on the way back to the orphanage.

"Come in," Mrs. Swen urged. She disappeared momentarily and came back with a tiny, crocheted baby bonnet. "It's for him," she said, "his first cap."

I took it, smoothing it in my hands. I tucked it carefully in the drawer when we reached home. "His very first piece of clothing," I told John; he turned away without answering. "Don't worry, darling," I said, "we're going to take good care of him."

At a knock John opened the door. The Rances stood there with a woman we had never seen before. "Mrs. Ames," Mr. Rance said. "She arrived while you were gone."

We shook hands. "I'll make coffee," I said. But Mr. Rance shook his head.

"She'll take over the orphanage as soon as the Swens leave. In the meantime, she's to be our guest."

Then that was settled! I glanced at her huge body and stony face. She didn't look as if she'd be settled long with anyone! I felt anxious all over again. Were we to become embroiled once more, with only a change in characters?

"Time will tell," said John as we got ready for bed. "All we can do is hope for the transfer."

On the last day of school we took the children on a picnic. We played games and ran races. For over seven months we'd worked together—their shyness turning to companionship, their chatter and quiet laughter mingling with our love and respect. John and I had worked to give them something of our life at home. We had struggled with the puzzle of presenting a strange world in words they would understand. And now, trudging the hillside, the children stayed close to us, slowing to our pace. For these, the first children we taught, understood our loneliness in a lonely land.

We walked through the roughness of the tundra. I looked down at the bright braids of the two little Eskimo girls, Laura and Virginia, at my side. The months had drawn these children close to my heart. They and the little ones ahead had come to my desk, their beautiful eyes alert, their smiles beguiling. When I rested, my head on the desk, they stood by, small in stature but great in sympathy.

This hour could never come again, for such hours are for the present; in another day, in another month, all would be changed, for these children would never pause in their growth. It would always be like this. We loved and we let go, and some of these little ones, trotting so blithely ahead, we might lose forever. At our door at last, gently, we released the last clinging hand.

John dropped into a chair. "The last day of school," he said. "And instead of feeling relieved, I feel depressed."

"I could crawl into bed right now," I agreed. "But isn't this the night the Swens are leaving?"

John nodded, worried. "The ice is too dangerous."

"But what'll they do? They resigned as of today."

A knock came at the door, and Mr. Swen entered, his face lined with weariness. He would not stay. "Haven't time," he said. "We're leaving at midnight." He glanced toward the river, the lines on his face deepening. "It's a long way to Nome on dangerous ice."

"You'll go by way of Solomon?" John asked.

"Yes, Joe's taking us. Says he knows the country . . ."

Joe, the foolhardy daredevil. John moved uneasily. "Ali says the days seem warmer than they are, and if you get wet—well, that's when men freeze to death."

The river's ditches must be crossed. Out on the trail, swirling waterholes developed when eddies and whirlpools ate away the melting ice. Hidden "honeycomb" ice lay in wait for the unwary.

"You could stay with us until the river thaws," John offered.

But Mr. Swen said, "We're leaving at twelve-thirty."

We played cards to while away the hours until midnight. On our way to the Swens we shivered in our parkas. "This is the best time of day to go," Mrs. Swen said in greeting, "because the ice is frozen." She looked toward the orphanage, toward the village.

I put my arm through hers. "The orphanage is a monument to your efforts. It'll be there many years, to remind everyone of all you've done. I'll never forget how kind you've been."

It was time to settle on the sled. She put her arms around me. "Take care of yourself," she said, "and let me know."

I felt sudden tears. The Swens had been nearly our age. They had been closest to us from the first. Now the world seemed a little lonelier.

As Joe stepped to the back of the sled, we were startled to find Mr. Rance standing beside us, staring tight-lipped.

Joe yelled, "Mush!" Mr. Rance strode away. John and I watched until we could no longer see the racing team.

At the door we looked once more at the trail.

"Maybe someday, somewhere, she'll see our baby."

Because the close of school did not mark the end of our year's contract, we were pleased when Mr. Rance told us we could take two weeks before starting our other duties.

Watching the ducks wheel overhead, John grinned eagerly. "We'll go hunting," he cried.

We gathered supplies for a two- or three-day trip. John packed blankets, food, his gun and shells in a canvas, and I packed the rest of the food in a haversack which I would carry, leaning backward slightly to balance the baby. The day was bright and warm. The thrill of a camping trip and the feeling of escape from village troubles pepped us up. After lunch we started along the banks of the river, going up and down its hills, sinking deep into the tundra, sometimes all but stumbling into hidden wells of water. Our feet were wet, but still we plodded on, singing the old songs as the hours passed. The sack on my back became heavier, the cans of food gouged deeper. My legs began to ache protestingly. Still, I wouldn't stop. When John halted to look through field glasses, I rested against a sapling, but when he started again I was ready to go on.

The weight of pregnancy forced me to go more slowly. Finally I could no longer keep up. John stopped at once.

"We'll make camp right here. Should be ducks close."

He built a fire in the shelter of spindly cottonwoods, then unrolled the canvas and blankets. "Here," he said, "lie down and rest. You looked dog-tired."

I stretched my stiff back. As the evening chill increased, we huddled under the blanket. Suddenly John sat upright, feeling our bedding.

"Wet!" he said. "Even the canvas is saturated! We can't possibly sleep in a place like this!"

So we reluctantly started out again. My back muscles stabbed me at every step now.

"Just a little bit further," John urged.

Finally we came to a brook protected by saplings. While John gathered wood, I unpacked the food once more, and spread the blankets for the night. After gulping cheese and pilot crackers, we crept under the sheltering blankets. All through the long, bitter night the cold dampness made us miserable. Under the bedding, hills and valleys, rocks and sticks threatened every bone in our bodies. In the small hours of the morning we finally slept, our faces buried in blankets.

When we woke, the brook was frozen solid. While I fixed breakfast John climbed one of the trees to have a look at the country through binoculars. He came back for his gun, ignoring the food that we were both too miserable to eat.

"I'll be back soon," he said.

He crept slowly toward the flats. Shortly after, I heard shots. Almost immediately he returned, grinning broadly, a large goose tied to each side of his belt.

"John!" I cried in delight, in spite of my chattering teeth.

He forgot his kill instantly. "Dolly," he said, "you're frozen! We'll start for home right now!"

"I don't believe I was ever meant to be a pioneer!"

John shouldered most of the load. "That leaves you only the baby!" He grinned. "Say, how about a feather mattress for him from all the birds I get?"

At my nod we swung happily to the trail.

Chapter 8

A WEEK LATER we heard a strange rumbling sound and rushed to the window. A vast quiver shook the river's surface; there was an ear-splitting crescendo of noise. The giant quilt of ice screamed for its life. A great shout of awe rose from the village as the mighty river, after months of captivity, strained and tore at ice-roots buried deep. The deafening roar continued. Gigantic ice masses splintered and plunged into formidable whirlpools of angry water.

The river began rising rapidly, spreading across the flatlands, crushing saplings, uprooting trees and tearing away the banks.

Mr. Rance, joining us to watch, raised his voice over the thunder. "Must be an ice jam out on the Bay."

"How long will it keep up?" I asked.

He watched the river. "Hard to tell. Depends on the wind. If it changes, it could sweep the ice out at once. Or it could hold it there." His thin lips clamped shut.

The ice picked up momentum. Mr. Rance sighed. "Thank heavens! Last year it took some dog teams and it nearly drowned one of the villages downstream."

John put his arm across my shoulder. "All the same, it's a magnificent sight!"

When dusk drove us indoors, we sat at the window, unwilling to forgo this splendor. And when darkness fell, John turned from the window, tilting my face up to his. "You don't look a bit different," he said. He grinned at my question. "Don't you know we've just passed another milestone? First we saw the freeze and now we've seen the break-up. What does that spell?"

"We qualify as sourdoughs!" I spread my hands in a dramatic sweep. "Having left behind the world of the green *cheechakos,* we join the exclusive club of Tom the squaw man and John the trader." We grinned and listened to the tumult.

"As soon as the water is open, I'm going to get some of those duck eggs the Eskimos seem to like. Wouldn't a fresh egg taste good?"

I gulped a bit at the thought. "How will you know if it's fresh?" I met his glance of merriment. "Just be sure they're not hatching!"

The opening of the Bay was like spreading wide the gates of freedom. Our whole outlook changed: no more did the river's ice imprison us. Now we could hike where we pleased; we could travel by kayak.

We walked to the river's edge. Putting the kayak into the water, John motioned for me to climb in. I backed away. "No," I said. "Even if I did manage to crawl into it, how could I ever get out again?"

"I borrowed it just for us. A kayak built for two. Come on and try it," he urged.

While John steadied the small sealskin boat, I stepped in cautiously. I bent my knees but couldn't find a way to fit the biggest part of myself within the kayak. With John's help I skidded ungracefully through the hole.

"These flimsy things were never made for pregnant women," I moaned.

John laced the cover about me and climbed into the second hole. Paddling first on one side and then the other, he swept us to midstream. Gradually, with the rhythmic sweep of his shoulders, the sun bursting warmly and the quiet sound of the dipping oar, joy and peace overwhelmed us. A sense of adventure hung in the air, hovering above the untrammeled banks, hiding in the untamed foothills. John, feeling it, began to sing. It was as unconquered tribesmen, as if we were people out of history come to see this new land, that we set out.

But it didn't last. My back throbbed, my numbed legs prickled, and the baby seemed to creep under my ribs.

I moved cautiously; the kayak swayed. John swung about. "Be careful," he warned, "or you'll dump us both."

Arriving, we pulled the kayak to the beach, then hiked and finally slithered toward the feeding grounds. "We're sure to find ducks on this side of the river," John assured me. The tundra was wet but we paid no heed—ahead were ducks!

We crept closer. John motioned toward the pond. There before us sat beautiful mallards, their green heads glistening, their tails a-curl.

John handed me the gun. I shook my head firmly. I didn't like to shoot; besides I was soaked and cold and uncomfortable, kneeling there. But he loaded the gun, put it into my hands and helped me aim.

"Now!" he whispered.

I pulled the trigger, keeping my eyes shut. I felt a terrific thud against my shoulder and found myself lying flat on my back. For a moment I could only look up at the sky and wonder what had pained me so. I turned my eyes beseechingly toward John. He came over and pulled me upright.

"What in the world happened?" I asked, feeling my chest to see if I was still whole. A slow grin came over John's face as he brushed me off, and the grin deepened into uncontrolled laughter. I couldn't see anything funny in being knocked to the ground. His laughter made me furious.

"That bump," he said, "was the gun. It kicked you a little as you pulled the trigger."

"A little! Do you call knocking me flat on my back a little?"

He was instantly contrite. "But you did get a duck!" he gloated. For a moment, I didn't want a duck or any of its brothers, but when he brought it to me I was very proud.

"All yours," he said. "And some feathers for the baby's bed. Aren't you pleased with yourself?"

I smiled. But I knew I'd never try hunting again.

At our return Tina stood in her doorway, hands folded at her thickened waist. She had been crying.

John went to her. "Tina, tell us. What's happened?"

She turned her round face toward him. "Big Jim, he go out to Bay to hunt seal. He not come back."

"In a kayak?" John asked.

She nodded. "He not come back."

"You can't be sure, Tina. He may be only late."

She shook her head. "He not late. They get caught in ice in Bay. They work and work to get back to shore, but the wind he come stronger and take him back into ice. Tom see them come close, close, and then he see them go out again, way out. Tom try to call. He not see them any more."

The tragedy left us cold and shocked. "I can't believe it," John said. "They've hunted like that for years. They know the dangers of the ice."

"John," I said, reaching for his hand, "you've got to be more careful!"

He looked at me sharply. "What's it got to do with me?"

"Everything! The ice, the river, the snow, the hunting—it's all dangerous!"

But the disappearance of Jim didn't lessen John's hunting fever. On Saturday afternoon we planned an overnight trip downriver to the mudflats with some of the children.

John looked down at me as we packed our food. "If I thought these trips——" He searched my face for reassurance.

"It'll be fun," I told him. "Come. We're late."

With canvas tarpaulin, blankets and food we set out, glad to be on our way. The afternoon on the river was hazy. We sat in peace, reviewing recent events in the white colony. "Mrs. Ames's methods are heading for trouble," John said. "She stopped me the other day to ask what she should do about Mr. Rance—and who should stalk by but the boss himself!" He watched the children in front of the boat. "It doesn't matter what I say, it could be miscontrued."

The wind rose and swept the water. Overhead a duck wheeled and settled gracefully. "Don't let's talk about them any more," I said.

Relaxing, we felt the deep chug-chug of the motor. We dozed in the silence of the flatlands, the purple hills, the soft sky.

Toward the mouth of the river the boat hove to and we carried our supplies ashore. We located our tent carefully; this was spring, the tundra still wet with the seepage of winter and the river high.

While the others went hunting, I lay quiet; relaxed in luxury, hearing the gentle lap of water and the call of geese.

When John and the boys returned with their birds, we ate and talked. One by one we slid into blankets. Sleep came fitfully; the bed was uneven, our covers much too skimpy. During the night a violent windstorm rose. Our tent, never too well fastened in the wetness, began to sway and lean with every gust of wind. In the darkness the boys found the anchor ropes and tried to tether the tent more firmly, but the wind whipped the ropes.

A heavy rain joined the wind, pouring down the sides of the leaning tent and racing in mad little creeks under and around us. As we huddled in the wetness, the tent abruptly collapsed. The boys tried to right it, but it was no use. The wind grabbed the canvas and the tent billowed over us again.

We huddled shivering, waiting for the dark to slide away. At times I sat under the fallen tent, unable to bear the exhausting weight, too miserable to see anything but the gray mist hanging low over rain-filled mudflats. All our supplies were wet, our matches, the food—and still the rain fell.

The high river, under the urging of the wind, slopped closer; waves sprayed more water toward us. Our whole world was fast becoming a nightmare of angry water. John came over and sat beside me. He was very wet and very cold. "John," I chattered, "what if the ice in the Bay dams the river? It could flood the whole country!"

He took my hand and warmed it. He saw my shivering body, my soggy shoes. And then he looked back to the churning river. He stood up and said, "You shouldn't sit in the damp too long."

The rain spattered his face, ran down his cheeks, dripped off his chin. He leaned far out into the mistiness.

"John——"

"Darling, look at that dot——" He pointed far in the distance. We strained to see a dot that came—and disappeared—and came again.

A mist sprang to my eyes, blurring the speck in the troughs of the waves. Our rescuers had arrived.

We gathered our supplies and quickly were hoisted aboard. After hot coffee I lay back, not minding the fishy smell of the blanket, the odor of sealskin, not even the lurching of the little boat. We were safe from the angry river. All else was insignificant. I looked over at John, tired and weary from the strain of the trip and then I closed my eyes. "Thank you, God," I said.

When we reached home, I asked John why the boat had come back for us. "They worried, once the storm began. They knew we weren't used to Arctic squalls."

We finished our soup in silence.

The next day, as we went to church, John seemed preoccupied and often he gazed without seeing the river or hearing the yelping dogs.

During the service I heard his voice, steady and sure, but afterward, going up the path, I felt his silence.

I reached for his arm. "What's wrong today? Are you worried about something?"

He tucked my hand in his. "Not a thing. I have a premonition and I can't place it."

Later, we ate in the living room before the window. There was fresh duck, roasted and stuffed, and Jello for dessert. We were grateful; no one yet knew when the first boat would arrive with food. If we were to be transferred, then our supplies would go to the new station. We were writing letters when the knock came. As if he knew, John opened the door. Mr. Rance handed him a telegram.

Closing the door at last, John turned to me. "It's from the Bureau." For a moment the room seemed very still. "Transferred," he read aloud, "to Pilot Station, Yukon River. Leave July." He looked up, dazed.

I read the telegram slowly. The problems of the future that

had been only a possibility crowded upon us, and some of the joy we'd anticipated turned to uneasiness.

We went back to the letters but neither could write. "It means we'll have to order more supplies——" But I knew John wasn't thinking about the extra food, the packing. He was thinking about the baby and the perils of a delayed journey. July was very nearly August, and we could not be sure the baby would not be born before the date we thought it might be due.

John put his pen aside, and I understood his quietness. There was the reindeer herd to supervise, medical work, school to teach and all the village activities to oversee. There would be no nurse or superintendent. We would be alone at Pilot Station.

There was no measurement by which to judge the life ahead of us. Still, we did not feel fear; only wonderment. We were on the verge of something we could not quite grasp. We groped for the familiar.

"It'll be days before we know how and when we are to go, how long the trip will take, how big a settlement it is."

"At least we know we're leaving here," I said. "Tomorrow we'll make out a larger grocery list."

"We ought to plan our trip to Council and Ophir Creek, if we're going." John looked at me. "Are you sure you're up to such a trip?"

"Why shouldn't I be able to stand it? The other trips didn't hurt me!"

"But late June will put you pretty far along. A trip by scow upriver and the overland trip to the creek—well, I'm wondering if we should attempt it."

"If we're going, we ought to go. It's our last chance," I said.

With the passing days I admitted my increasing clumsiness. When John hunted, I stayed home, making out lists for the winter. I added many luxury items we had omitted last year, for we had learned that without these few consolations our life was too bleak. We ordered a gunnysack of mixed nuts, buckets of various candies, cartons of cookies. Everything we'd craved these last frugal months would not be amiss another year! Neither would sewing materials nor warmer clothes. Included in the list, as much at my urging as his, was an outboard motor for John.

But the weeks often dragged in spite of my efforts. Sometimes I stood at the windows, longing for human companionship yet not daring to seek out our neighbors, for with our leaving we wanted more than ever to avoid last-minute complications.

At last word came that the *Victoria*, loaded with her first cargo from Outside, was due in Golovin. There would be the winter's accumulation of papers and packages. There would be food and clothes. And there would be letters.

At Ivory Pete's we bought letter openers and napkin rings; from Tina, skinning knives and reed baskets. We found an ivory cribbage board and bought an ivory doll for the baby.

One morning we sighted the scow returning from Golovin. We rushed to the landing, our hearts hammering. With this boat came the first real touch with the Outside.

When the scow beached, we watched as boxes, cartons and packages were unloaded. Our arms filled with belated Christmas packages and letters, we climbed back to the little house. Sitting side by side we opened the letters and began reading aloud.

The isolation, the inconveniences, the cold, the mosquitoes— even the coming birth—did not haunt us. We had each other and a job to do. All the rest we could take in our stride. Even letters from those we loved, even our homesickness—and we were homesick—made us turn to each other and be comforted; the horizon of life itself stopped there.

And so, putting the letters away, we made ready for the journey to Council and Ophir. When the scow appeared far down the river, we shouldered our supplies and adjusted the mosquito netting around our heads and faces. Stepping aboard the scow, we found a place to stand. Horses were aboard to pull us over the shallow riffles.

The boat moved upstream. The steep banks we'd hiked along, the river we'd skated across, the little island in the center—we chugged noisily past them all. Our spirits rose like the smoke ascending from the fish-drying racks along the shore. It was summer. It was brilliantly sunny. The hills in the distance were emerald green. The horses, big and brown, stood motionless and snorted in their dreams. The pilot stood at his post, steering the clumsy craft and watching the river ahead. The few passengers pulled their caps down over their eyes and slept.

"Why don't you try to sleep?" John asked. "We won't be stopping for hours." John found an extra coat and smoothed it over some of the boxes. "Here," he said, "lie down."

Ahead, riffles danced over shallow rocks. The scow moved toward the bank; the harnessed horses were led from the deck to the bank and the towlines were adjusted.

"We'll soon be pulling to shore for the night," John said. "How do you feel?"

"Fine. It'll be good to rest awhile."

He held my hand. "Imagine what a sight the river must have been in the days of the gold-seekers! Scows like this full of lumber for the hotels, cafés, saloons, dance halls, rooming houses!"

"And furniture, supplies, food."

Ahead was a small clearing. The scow turned slowly, and we felt the pull of the current. Dusk was lowering, the hills were turning a powdery purple and blue; soft smoke gathered in the hollows. We could see the faint outline of a building on the slope. Abandoned years before, it stood alone, unvisited except by people like us who must have a place to stay the night. Unpainted, dark, its battered door creaked open; the bare floors sagged beneath our tread.

In the kitchen the huge black range made me wonder how many sourdough pancakes, loaves of fragrant bread, gallons of steaming coffee had been cooked here. Dishes, stacked in the cupboard, were veined with a thousand cracks; below, stored every which way as men would leave them, were knives, forks and spoons. A coffeepot, chipped and stained, stood on the stove's high warming closet.

The crew knew the duties of those who stopped here—leave things as they found them, replenish anything that had been used. Before long the meal was ready and coffee bubbling in the pot. I did as much as I could but I felt inexperienced and clumsy with these capable men, who spared me all effort though I felt no need of their solicitude.

After the meal of canned stew, I cleared the table and washed the dishes as others had done before us. At last, too tired to sit up, John and I crawled into the creaking, sagging bed, wondering if adventurers and their ladies had died on it, if gold and firearms and the fear and treachery which accompany them had lain down here before us.

John reached over and gave me a gentle pat. "Go to sleep," he admonished. "Tomorrow's another hard day!"

Long after he'd gone to sleep, I listened to the whispers of the old building.

We rose early. Already, stepping aboard the boat, I knew the mosquitoes would not bother me so much today, for old Smithy had assured me that though mosquitoes could bite through many things, paper defeated them, and we had old paper to wrap about my legs. Much to my relief, he was right.

We spent the day dreaming of this great river, as a trail during the Gold Rush—racing dog teams in the bitter cold, men lost, frozen. We remembered the skeleton we had found the month before, propped against a big rock, pan and pick by its side. Snow and ice had covered it. We wondered who the man might have been.

"No one will ever know. Maybe no one ever missed him."

On that day we'd been hiking far from the village. Finding the remains of the skeleton had been like stumbling into the presence of death.

At once, the memory of the skeleton became a symbol to us of all the men who must lie under the snow and ice along the trail across the reaches of the tundra. We knew how some had died—quickly, violently. The man confused when a howling blizzard darkened the sky and hid all landmarks; his dog team had fought; the dogs turned on him, their master, and all had perished. For some there had been riches, greed and instant death. For others the saloons, gambling, the treachery of sly friends. And for some there had been the perils of ideals, of vibrant hopes, of weak bodies.

We slapped at the droning mosquitoes; heard the horses prance; felt the current tug at the soft, swishing, bottled-up gurgling of the disturbed water; looked up, startled, at the flicker of swift wing-beats overhead—and never quite dispelled the enchantment of the violent past.

After lunch John said, "You ought to rest before we get to

Council. We'll want to visit everything from saloon to dance hall!"

"We will," I promised.

Council, once a mighty and lustful settlement, lay forsaken. The buildings were in all stages of decay, according to the haste with which they had been built; some stood wretched and stained and sad; some sagged and buckled on tottering foundations; other stood gaunt and scarred like proud and aged queens. But all had been forsaken.

We turned as Tom, the squaw man, came toward us with outstretched hand. We had promised to visit him. We followed him through the silent town to a house at some distance, a house larger than most native homes. An Eskimo girl, holding a baby on her back, smiled shyly. Tom said, "This is Lucy, my wife."

Tom showed us the house. "This is a relic of the Rush, too. Someday the snow will finish tearing off the porch."

We sat at an oilcloth-covered table, pleased to have the relaxing coffee, the hot biscuits and jam. But we could not rest long, for the day was ending and all around us lay a sense of the past.

Halting at the first of the crumbling buildings, Tom seemed to be recalling the nakedness of the birth of this frontier town. He seemed to live again the spell of the fever, the gold-hunger that gnawed at men until they murdered for it. He looked at us, his eyes unseeing. Abruptly he pushed his gnarled fingers through his hair, and when he met our look the yesterdays had vanished. "It all went up so fast—the saloons, the dance halls, the eating places. You never saw the like. Men worked day and night to have a share in the riches."

"Judging from the number of saloons, most of the miners must have been thirsty men," John said.

"They liked their liquor, most any liquor, I guess. And the gals—there were plenty of gals up here."

"Ophir Creek must have been paved in gold to attract such a crowd as this place handled. Gold must have been as easy to find as gravel."

"No," Tom said, "not for everybody it wasn't. If we go on up to Ophir tomorrow, you'll see some of the dredges still there."

We continued along the board sidewalk, opening sagging doors, peering through smoke-smudged windows.

Tom reached into his pocket, pulling out a chain of keys. "You can't see it all unless you go inside one or two; leastways, we don't think so." He began sorting the array of keys in his hand. "Lots of times we come here just to gawp and stare. Seems we never get used to it." He pushed the door wide, motioning us to follow. Inside, we stood motionless, yesterday's grandeur, yesterday's history, overwhelming us. We turned to Tom, trying to comprehend what lay swathed in dust before us.

He shook his head at the question on our faces. "I know 'tisn't right," he said, moving ahead, "but 'tisn't anybody's fault that it's lying here in rot."

We moved slowly behind him, our voices stilled by the emptiness. Tom spoke: "Me and my wife like to stand here—and just look."

Worn carpets softened our footsteps; faded draperies hung at the windows; a great piano, beautiful even under decades of dust, sat mute, waiting; sheet music had spilled in a cascade from the piano top to the bench as though the player had jumped up a moment before. I sat down in the dust and fingered the keyboard, untouched for years; the sounds reverberated and died in the hollow, desolate room. John reached down to recover the music, but his hand paused as he touched it; he straightened, leaving it as it had been.

Somewhere close—in this room or the next—the dancing girls must have been shimmying and shaking for the promise of gold glittering in every eye, and somewhere—in the rooms upstairs— women in low-cut gowns were teasing for nuggets to hide between their breasts or tuck in the tops of their stockings.

We followed Tom to the stairs. Before us spread the bar; we paused, staring at the abandoned, glittering scene, catching our breath at the sight of the wasted magnificence. The bar stood huge and long and beautiful. Above it hung large mirrors reflecting through their dusty expanse open shelves lined with goblets, with wineglasses, with the myriad appurtenances of a successful enterprise. Towels hung below the counter; soap was covered with feathers of dust; silver, dishes, coffeepots and used aprons—it was all there.

We turned to Tom. "It's as if they were still expected—as if tonight the men would come bursting in."

We sat down on dusty stools, transfixed by the unreality of the scene, imagining the tinkling of crystal chandeliers, the shimmering of gold nuggets, the flaring candlelight. "Why in the name of heaven would they leave all this?" John asked. "There must be thousands of dollars worth of furnishings!"

Tom rolled a cigarette. "You've never seen a gold strike. 'Tisn't like anything else in the world! Men died here. Some got rich out there in the creek. Others got rich by playing it smart." He nodded at the splendor.

I touched the little glasses, the silver, wishing desperately that I could take them with me, but knowing I could not.

Rising, Tom led us to another broad stairway.

Upstairs, door after door lined the hall. "You see!" Tom said and grinned as we gasped. Piles of linen, still folded, lay neatly on the shelves. I touched the dozens and dozens of yellowing sheets, pile upon pile of pillowcases. Further down the hall, storage cupboards of tablecloths and napkins; in still another closet, brooms, dustpans and cleaning supplies.

We stood amid these riches and felt as a Midas must feel, with splendor everywhere and all of it useless.

Another door, larger than the others, Tom opened with a flourish. "It might be a mite dusty, but the room's all yours for tonight if you want it."

We paused on the threshold, breathing the stale air that billowed forth. "We can stay here?" John asked.

Tom nodded, happy that he had pleased us. "Been years since a maid fixed that bed . . ." He smiled, his eyes suddenly warm.

John thanked him. "We can't tell you how much this day means. We'll see you in the morning. Thanks a million!"

"For breakfast," Tom said, and we nodded.

When Tom's footsteps died away, we settled in chairs, forgetting the dust. "I feel like pinching myself to make sure I'm not dreaming." I examined the bed. "Why, there's not a wrinkle on it, not one!"

"I do believe the maid just left," John said nonsensically. He came to my side. "Do you suppose these sheets will be strong enough to last the night? They've lain here waiting for us a long, long time!"

We got out of our shirts, trousers, shoes and socks. We crept under the clean, slightly dusty blankets; we snuggled close.

The night was not night at all. Even the drawn blinds could not keep out the Alaskan twilight. Weary as we were, neither of us could sleep. It was as if our weary bodies took up the pulse of history around us; as if the grizzled and begrimed, the feverish and the stubborn were not gone at all, but waiting to return the moment we slept. It was as if the dancing girls, the thudding piano, the crescendo of voices only waited for some magic touch to awaken them. We seemed in a place out of time, trespassing in a dimension few are allowed to visit.

I moved closer to John. I put my arm across him. I felt the loneliness of this fantastic room, the eeriness of our sleeping here where no one had slept for decades.

John took my hand. The staleness of the blankets exhaled with his movement. "Relax, Dolly," he said. "Tomorrow's trip won't be easy for you."

I closed my eyes against the twilight, against the quiet that hovered in the shadows, the corridors. He was right. I must try to sleep. Sleep would lull the dull ache of my back. And sleep would quiet the movements of our baby. I held John's hand tighter, aware of the life within me so dependent on my own. All must go well on this trip! I moved my hand and felt the sigh of the brass bed.

In the morning yesterday's weariness was gone. John went to the window, looking from the settlement to the far hills.

"Sometimes I think we're crazy, you and I," he said.

"At least, we never know what's coming next."

He came back to bed, pulling the sheet taut, anchoring the yellowed blankets. I leaned back against his chest and looked at the early sun. Out there was another day and new people and places to see. Behind us lay the familiar little red house. I shook my head. We must be up and on our way.

I sat down once more in the frayed armchair, touching the dust-laden tapestry. And knowing that one day the chair would crumble. Then we left the room and went along the empty hall. This feeling of emptiness would haunt us.

"I've been in lots of vacated houses," John said, "but this silence, with signs of life everywhere, makes me think of Biblical times, when whole towns were abandoned as they stood. You remember seeing pictures of people running, leaving everything behind? Pompeii. Still, it isn't quite like that either."

Downstairs, we lingered for a moment and then we left the hotel.

Chapter 9

THE MEN WERE LOADING the supplies for Ophir Creek. Something resembling an outmoded boxcar stood on narrow-gauge railroad tracks. John and I watched with puzzled interest. "It has no engine," John said, "but it certainly can't make that hill without something to pull it!"

Just then a team of malemutes was brought over and hitched to the little train. We climbed aboard. Miraculously the train began to move, gained momentum and reached the top of the slope without difficulty. The dogs were then unhitched and the train traveled downgrade alone.

Nearing Ophir Creek we saw great dredges standing in the midst of gouged-out river gravel and in isolated ponds. All around, the earth had been shoveled and reshoveled, the great gravel banks torn asunder and the creek dammed.

We were met by the Ellises, who still mined the creek, and others who came to Ophir Creek with the spring thaw and left when the creek froze.

"What a tremendous job!" John said.

Mr. Ellis pushed back his hat. "That it is," he agreed. "We have to do a full year's work in the few weeks of summer!"

Mrs. Ellis led the way to the cookhouse. "What you need is a cup of coffee. And there's pie to tide you over till dinner."

John came in, still questioning Mr. Ellis. "Didn't the big companies clean out all the gold before they left?"

"Not all of it. I ran one of the dredges for them. Now and again the dredge covered up some of the gold. I tried to recollect where the places were, and when the big boys left, I stayed on."

After finishing the pie, we inspected the huge dredges. Because it was Sunday, the men weren't working, but we could see how the shovels dug deep into the banks of the creek as the buckets revolved up and over on a continuous chain.

"You'll have to try panning for gold," Mrs. Ellis said. And so the next morning our host showed us how to scoop up a mixture of sand and water, how to tilt and swish and shake the pan again and again, until only the gold—or nothing—was left. We panned excitedly for an hour and a half, then followed Mr. Ellis to the weighing house to see how much gold we had collected.

"Worth about a dollar and a half!" he said, grinning, and put the gold into a bottle. "Take it home for the baby. Someday you'll be tellin' her about this trip!"

At the end of the visit, Mrs. Ellis kissed my cheek. "You got someone to take care of you when the time comes?"

I shook my head. Her motherly kiss reminded me of home. "We're leaving for the Yukon almost as soon as we get back."

Her kindliness sent me yearning for my mother's solicitude. I wanted to hear her say, "It's going to be all right, darling." Instead, I turned away to hide my tears.

During the following days plans for the transfer absorbed every waking hour. Memories of the past months were poignant as we began the labor of packing. At last, after everything was loaded on the waiting boat, after the Eskimos had crowded close to say good-by, we walked up the hill for the last time to look at the house in which we'd lived. The bedroom with its iron bedstead, the storage room, the kitchen with its stove and empty water bucket, our beloved organ . . . Gently we closed the creaking door. Every step down the hill helped us to remember the events we were about to leave behind.

From the boat, far out on the river, we watched the village fade from sight. Our many friends stood waving, the dogs howled and whimpered, and then suddenly there was only the chugging of the motor. Ahead lay Pilot Station.

At Golovin we waited endless days for the boat to St. Michael. When at last the boat arrived, John and I joined the excited villagers, all our worries of waiting, of indecision, of wondering, resolving at once, until we were like a dammed-up river spilling over the countryside. We were glad to leave the leaning porch of the miner's house where we'd spent endless hours. Now, in the space of a breath, our stay at Golovin was over.

We met the friendliness and curiosity of the passengers on board the ship with a sudden shyness. When they asked questions, we couldn't satisfy them, for so many of the things we'd seen couldn't be put in words.

After dinner we relaxed in our stateroom. I said, "If you want to go on deck——"

John shook his head; he seemed troubled. "No more than you do. It's queer—for months we've been alone and lonely. And now——"

As we neared St. Michael, a doctor on board stopped us briefly. He was amazed and worried that I should be traveling so close to the end of my term. He admonished us to make careful provisions for the baby's birth, saying that the possibility of infection must not be ignored. We promised wholeheartedly to do all in our power to safeguard the coming child and my own health.

St. Michael was a town of many empty houses and buildings, of rusting paddle-wheelers, all that was left of a time when boats raced up the mighty Yukon, when freighters docked to load great fortunes in gold.

Even our musty hotel room's threadbare rug and scarred furniture appeared to echo another age. We set out to see the town before darkness settled, visiting the old Russian fort, the church, the telegraph station. We bought beautifully carved ivory cribbage boards, dolls and jewel boxes as gifts on our way back to the hotel.

Later, across the dinner table, we were introduced to a couple who immediately made us welcome.

"You're the teachers who are taking our place at Pilot! We're on our way back to the States."

"To stay?" I exclaimed.

John said, "How long will we have to wait for a boat up-river?" But they were not sure. Perhaps a week.

"Is there a woman at Pilot Station who can help me when the baby comes?" I asked.

No, there wasn't, except the teacher at Russian Mission, three days' travel by launch from Pilot.

"You must know her," they said, "Bertha Keyes. She has a little girl. You met on the ship from the States."

Bertha, who was afraid to say "yes," to the widower Bill, was still alone. But Russion Mission was a long way from Pilot Station.

Then we were told of an ex-nurse who lived with her husband miles up the Yukon and some six miles overland on foot through

tundra plagued by mosquitoes and *nosee-ums*. And there was a
hospital boat which came down the river once each season. The
only other hope was the hospital on the Kuskokwim River. To
reach it would mean a journey many miles upriver and a hike
overland to Kuskokwim, carrying a skin boat to cross the inter-
vening sloughs and ponds. How long would the trip take? It
would depend upon the rain, the river, the sloughs. We would
need a guide. There would be no shelter at night. If the ponds
and lake were nearly dry the hiking would be worse because
boats would be useless. It would be a terrible trip for one heavy
with child.

I slept badly that night, and so did John. Several days later
our boat arrived. The trip up the Yukon begins after some miles
of open sea. The mouth of the river spreads dark and shallow,
and boats must watch for the channel. Ours was a paddle-
wheeler; the turning wheel spoke to us as the boat churned toward the river mouth.

As we stopped at each little village to pick up and deliver
supplies, the riverbanks rose high or leveled out into flatlands
and brush. When the wind stirred up the swift current, all
boats made for sheltered coves. The river was heavy with silt.
"If you fall in," cautioned the pilot, "you're done for. The silt
drags you to the bottom." We stared at the waters racing brown
beneath us.

Before long we were approaching Pilot Station. We saw its
outline brighten. Others on board crowded near to watch us
disembark and see to our supplies. At last we stood on the bank
of the mighty river, looking up at a small green and white house
in which we were to live and teach.

We climbed a flight of wooden steps to the yard and pushed
open the front door. To the left, as we entered, was the school-

room; to the right, the living room. The living room windows faced the river. Upstairs there were two bedrooms and a storage attic over the schoolroom. Beyond the house rose somber hills looking down upon the Yukon.

The boat whistled. We went to the door and watched the boat pull away and fade into the distance as the current swept it into the channel.

It was quiet now and we were alone. John put his arms around me and held me close, and each of us thought our own thoughts. Suddenly John said, "What day is it?"

"July twenty-third," I said. How little time remained before the baby was due!

John found villagers to help him carry food, school supplies and clothing to the attic and the storage shed. Closets needed airing, the cupboards needed washing. Cooking utensils and dishes must be washed again before we felt settled in our new house. We worked from early morning until late at night. The villagers cut and hauled the winter's wood. Since we were to keep track of the weather, instruments were to be read and data recorded.

The government furnished us a flat-bottomed scow as a launch. The pilot, who would serve as an interpreter, was an Eskimo of mixed blood called Burt. As soon as the last supplies were on the shelves and other pertinent jobs attended to, we made arrangements to go upriver in quest of a nurse or mid-wife, with Burt as our guide.

"I don't think we can wait a day longer," John said. And I had reason to know he was right.

Our flat-bottomed scow chugged heavily along, sending blue smoke through the cabin. Inside, without room enough to stand

erect, I stooped over the tiny gas stove. The inconvenience did
not detract from the vision of high banks rising above the river,
the lushness of willows and cottonwood spreading far afield, the
soft murmur of a summer day. It was exhilarating to be alive—
to feel the freshness of the blue sky, cool breezes, complete relaxation. How people in the States would envy us this lazy day,
the total absence of noise and rush and tension! How those at
Blue Ridge—but I put away the thought. Here, at last, the
hours, the months, were our own. After lunch was over I
stretched out in the sun.

In the afternoon we reached Marshall, forty miles from Pilot.
Here were white traders, squaw men and a trading post. Here
also was the dog team owned by the teachers who had preceded
us. John dickered with the present owner and arranged to buy
five dogs and pick them up later.

But what we had hoped to find wasn't here. Mrs. Foster, the
ex-nurse, was at Willow Creek and would not return to Marshall
until the end of summer. There was no way to reach her except
by hiking six rough miles over tundra. I could only shake my
head in dismay at such a thought.

Perhaps Bertha at Russian Mission would help us. But the
men at Marshall tried to dissuade us from undertaking such a
trip.

"Unless you know what you're about, it's mighty dangerous
country," they warned us.

"How long will it take?" John asked.

"Two, three days, maybe more, depending on the weather."

John turned to me, but I did not want to make the decision.
The thought of hiking the miles to Willow Creek, across mos-
quito-swarming tundra, seemed an excruciating obstacle to
someone sagging under a baby's weight. But swift angry waters,

hungry whirlpools and an unfamiliar river left me as badly frightened of the journey to Russian Mission.

"It's up to you," I said at last. In the silence there was only the ticking of a clock. Thoughts raced through my mind— crazy thoughts of home, of a hospital, a doctor. For a moment I was there; gone the fear, the doubts, the backache; the river, the boat, the mosquitoes, the tundra. For a moment I was comforted.

John's big hand was warm on my shoulder. "If we don't go on——" He didn't finish. I nodded. There could be no other decision; we had to continue our search for a midwife.

The old trader drew us a map, showing the sheltered coves, the canyons, the depths. We shook hands and climbed aboard the boat. John and Burt took turns at the wheel. The sun and the breeze were warm and soft. I rested when time grew heavy, but for the most part I was aware of the growing anxiety of the men.

Repeatedly they scanned the sky. They watched the swaying bushes warily. They wiped the engine and listened to its heartbeat. Almost imperceptibly the wind shifted. A ripple tore up the current ahead. John and Burt straightened, meeting each other's glance. Burt pointed to the map. "It's not the cove. The cove is too far ahead."

The waves grew angrier; the wind whistled up the narrowing canyon. The boat rolled and shivered and hesitated at each pounding shock. I crowded close to John, feeling the thrust of the river's weight against the thin boards. I remembered John's uneasiness at going out in a flat-bottomed boat in rough weather. I looked at John, at the curling whitecaps ahead. Burt's face tightened as he clung to the wheel.

Ahead, the river narrowed. We crouched together, fastened

our lifebelts and watched the raging, silt-filled river. We were coming nearer the gorge. "It's going to be a rough haul," John shouted to me above the storm. "The boat can't take much more pounding like this——"

The pilot's words were in my thoughts: "If you fall into this river, you're done. The silt drags you to the bottom . . ."

Gradually, almost imperceptibly, we felt an easing of the shuddering boat. We stared at each other. John listened to the motor's throbs, Burt stared ahead into the whitecaps. We almost forgot to breathe as we waited for the thud of the waves against the bottom. For a time no one spoke. We were trembling in the ordeal of the moment.

"Look!" John called above the singing motor. Before us, the swaying trees were quietening, the whitecaps seemed less dangerous as the river widened. There was safety once more, the safety that follows the storm.

Late darkness was coming when we found Bertha at Russian Mission.

"How wonderful!" She was delighted to see us. "Come on up to the house."

We talked far into the night. But when we spoke of our errand, Bertha was disturbed. Fresh coffee gave neither of us stimulation. By morning it was clear that Bertha did not feel herself capable of helping us. Her fears were too great to be anything but a handicap.

Saying good-by to Bertha next day left us strangely relieved.

Once back at Marshall we asked about the overland trip to the Kuskokwim River and its hospital. But the old trader would not encourage our plan.

"You jes' can't make it!" he growled, peering over his glasses.

"Them ponds are bogs this summer, and the boats can't cross them. You'd wade in mud to your hips!" He shook his grizzled head. "You'd die tryin'! Here——" He pointed on a map to the miles of tundra and flatlands that separated the Yukon and the Kuskokwim rivers. "You can't hike that!"

There remained only Mrs. Foster, the nurse at Willow Creek. We left a letter for Mrs. Foster with the old trader at Marshall, asking if I might travel to Willow Creek during the first week in August to be with her during my confinement. After that, we put the perilous journey from our minds.

Chapter 10

ANXIOUS TO GET HOME, we traveled late; the twilight persisted in soft shadows over hills and water. The sun seemed never to dip beneath the horizon. Just before midnight the light was dim, not quite enough for reading. Then the shadows deepened around us and for a short time the earth slept. But it was no more than a momentary lessening of day, for as we arrived at Pilot Station it was dawn.

Upstairs in our new house I slipped out of my clothes. "No bed ever felt better." I pushed myself under the covers. "I don't think I'll ever want to get out of bed."

"But you will," John said, crawling in beside me. "The sun won't let us sleep long."

And it didn't. Nor did awareness of the work ahead of us. For in the first waking hour our thoughts concerned the jobs to be finished before our Willow Creek trip.

John made a crib and I sewed a mattress cover of denim and stuffed it with the feathers we'd saved. A few days later when the layette arrived, we unpacked the tiny shirts, diapers, slips and dresses. And abruptly I felt we couldn't wait any longer for the baby, we wanted the child so desperately.

119

John picked up one of the shirts. "I can't imagine him being so small!"

I smoothed the soft blankets. Here, shortly, the baby would lie, a tiny new life.

"I don't want to leave you now," John said, remembering that as one of his duties he must visit the reindeer herds. I looked across the gully to the village of huts separated from our house by a high footbridge. I'd met some of the villagers already— Laura, who lived with her husband's ailing parents and grandparents. I'd seen, from my kitchen window, a lame man drag himself to the doorway and the sunshine. I'd seen Mary the orphan and her brother Mat playing with a doll made of rags and wearing torn mukluks, the children chewing on bits of dried fish.

I turned to John. "I can call on them for help, if I need help while you're gone."

Another part of the village sprawled below us, close to the river's eddy. "We'll go visiting this afternoon," John said. "Perhaps there's someone there——"

After lunch we went down in a small boat. Many huts were still vacant, their owners off for a summer of fishing and hunting, but in others broad smiles welcomed us. The Eskimos here had little contact with white man, even less than those living at Blue Ridge.

We went first to the largest house in the village. An elderly white man wearing a toupee opened the door. Behind him stood his very young native wife, and close to her skirts were four or five little children, all of them quite fair-skinned and resembling their father.

The man stepped aside, smiling. "Come in—and welcome!

We're Henry and Grace Wills. You're the new teachers. Stay and have a cup of coffee."

We enjoyed watching the children. I was delighted to find that Grace Wills spoke English fairly well.

"I was an orphan at a mission upriver," she explained. "One day Henry came for a wife." She picked up the youngest child and pushed back his long hair. "You expecting soon?"

"About the middle of the month," I said. "Is there a woman who helps you?"

"Yes, but I've never had trouble."

We arranged that Grace and her friend Oolinga would come to help me if I were unable to make the trip to Willow Creek.

"We ought to go soon," John said later. "The sooner the better, for your sake. I don't know how much longer I can put off going to the reindeer camp. But I don't want to leave you."

"Will you have to stay overnight?"

"Perhaps two or three nights. That's what worries me." During his absence I would have to cross the footbridge and get Grace Wills or Laura if I needed help.

I put my arm through his. "Nothing will happen while you're gone. It's early for the baby. If you go the day after tomorrow, you'll be back in plenty of time for our trip to Willow Creek."

There was no other solution to the problem. John talked with the villagers who would be going along to slaughter reindeer for winter meat. We packed his blankets, extra clothing.

The boat pulled away and crossed into the swift current, sawing and chugging. Far across the river lay the dark slough they would follow to the reindeer camp.

I left the window then and turned to the housework. While

packing for John's trip, we had neglected the smaller household chores. I was grateful for the work that had to be done. After that came the task of checking and organizing the medicine closet. As representatives of the Bureau we had full responsibility, as had the other teachers, of administering to the sick as best we could. I studied the government medical books.

At Blue Ridge we'd learned something of our responsibilities while trotting at Miss Charles's heels. We knew our limitations and some of the dangers we might encounter. We had learned the value of such things as aspirin and various mild salves and disinfectants. But these shelves were lined with other medicines I knew nothing about.

In the medical book I read carefully the section on childbirth —about the sterilization of instruments, the necessity of scrubbing hands and nails and the types of pain inherent in childbirth. When evening came I tried not to think of my loneliness. I intended to light a lamp, but in the quiet house the noise of a match being struck would have been too loud, and so I crept into bed without it. For a long time I lay there feeling the gymnastics of the baby and easing the ache in my back as best I could.

I rose the next morning determined to accomplish much more, especially in the schoolroom. The day passed quickly enough. The sun stayed warm through the windows. Now and then I looked out at the slough, hoping the reindeer hunters would come back sooner than they were expected.

That night I climbed the stairs slowly, more clumsily than usual, for the baby seemed suddenly nearer birth than we thought. When I woke the next morning, I realized it was the third of August. The sun streamed through the window. Down in the States it would be sunny too. The hay would be fragrant in the barns; the fruit would be hanging firm and young. At home Mother would be planning Dad's birthday dinner. All day I tried not to expect the impossible. I tried not to go to the window or the door or listen for that familiar *chug-chug*. I baked cookies. I ate lunch. I willed myself not to look at the clock. I made toast and coffee. I ate beside the window, trying not to admit my restlessness. I lingered over another cup of coffee. I told myself I must go to bed, that it was too late for John to come. But the silence of another night was difficult to face.

I turned to the stair, to the room above. I undressed and went to the window and leaned a little closer to the pane. Had I heard a motor far out? The throb of the motor came again.

The next morning some of the strain had eased from my face. The sun had deepened the lines on John's forehead, had darkened his throat and neck. His whiskers were bristly and long. I held him close in deep gratitude.

"This is the day we pack for the trip to Willow Creek."

Breakfast was a gay affair, neither of us willing to admit how we disliked being separated. All day I cleaned and baked, John checked the boat's gas and refilled the stove.

I said, "It'll be wonderful to feel light as a feather once more!"

As we went up the stairs, John gave me an extra boost at the landing. "In the meantime, hop into bed and relax! That trip tomorrow makes me shudder."

An hour and a half later I woke. There was still light in the room and I raised to look at the time. Ten o'clock . . . I lay back and closed my eyes. Something far off had awakened me. A dog, disturbed in its sleep. I settled down. This was my last night at home. Then it came again. Not a noise in the village, but the first pain. For a moment I lay breathlessly, trying to pacify it. Unexpectedly it eased, and I exhaled in relief. It was only a passing thing—perhaps a result of overweariness. It was nothing. Why, the baby wasn't due for two weeks!

I turned on my back and closed my eyes against the breath of worry. As it subsided, I lay tense, realizing, yet not believing, that labor was upon me. I lay quietly, trying not to wake John. But John turned toward me, wide awake.

"Darling," he whispered, "what's wrong?" I could tell by the startled sound of his voice that he knew. He lit the lamp. "Do you think it's the baby?"

I nodded.

"I guess you didn't really want to take that trip tomorrow, did you?" He smiled at my smile.

I pressed his hands. "No," I said, "no, I really didn't." I turned away to hide another pain.

John began to dress. "I've got to get the baby's things out of the boat." He pulled on his socks and hunted for his shoes, which were in plain sight. "Will you be all right until I get back?"

I swung gracelessly to the edge of the bed.

"The doctor said——" He didn't finish the doctor's words of warning, but instead busied himself putting fresh sheets on the bed.

"What else did the book say?" John asked, steadying me. "You get back into bed. I'll look after everything."

"You'll have to go to the lower village and ask Grace to come," I told him.

Leaning over, he suddenly kissed me. Then he was gone. I heard him running down the walk to the boat. Now he would be climbing aboard, shoving off, starting the balky motor.

The quiet of the room deepened. Perspiring now with the

efforts of labor, I felt the moments of midnight pass. I thought of John and the help he would bring.

I turned again to watch the clock. A half hour had gone. Ten more minutes. Any moment now Grace and John would come. I closed my eyes; it wasn't as long as it seemed. The pain tightened. I struggled and lay back again. I thought of the village across the footbridge, but there was no one there to hear me call. My mind slipped back to the big brown house at home, to the fields and pastures and the shady banks where the horses came down to drink the cool water, to the creek that wound serenely through the leafy woods, to the orchard, to the kitchen, big and warm, with the richness of fragrant foods.

I must get to the window. I must look for John.

Holding first to the bed and then the chair, I reached the window.

Perhaps I should go down the stairs and across the bridge for help. I had begun to believe that John might not come back in time. And in that instant, as so often happens in a moment of crisis, the acceptance of what seemed inevitable calmed my fears.

Shivering, I crept back into bed. Somehow I'd manage.

Only fifteen minutes had passed but it might have been fifteen hours. The whole room seemed to center on the ticking clock. I began to count the ticks. One . . . two . . . three . . . five . . . ten . . . fifteen . . . And then suddenly its ticking mingled with a sound out of the night. Suddenly its rhythm broke, and I lay breathless.

Footsteps on the walk below. The front door creaked and slammed; someone came three steps at a time up the stairs; and then John was back.

"It's all right," I said; "everything's all right."

"I thought I'd never get here in time. I couldn't hold her steady in the high wind. I couldn't pull her out of the current."

"You're dead tired, darling. Go get some coffee."

But he shook his head. "Grace will be here soon. She's bringing Oolinga to help." Tenderly he brushed back my hair.

Just then we heard Grace and Oolinga on the stairs. Their cotton parka hoods were thrown back from round, impassive faces; black, braided hair hung to their shoulders.

Grace came to the bed, and Oolinga went with John to fetch hot water and soap. They timed the spasms of pain. Their whispers were low. They settled in the corner opposite the bed, silent in their parkas, their hands folded quietly, their dark eyes watchful.

Finally Grace spoke to John. "It is long coming. See, the morning is here!" John raised the blind. But the new day brought only clouds and wind.

Eight o'clock. Nine. Coffee steamed untouched beside me. "Oolinga say we must tie a cloth around her . . ."

But John shook his head. The weight of decision turned his face ashen.

Suddenly Grace spoke to John. "You must go now." They pushed him gently but firmly to the door.

Minute by minute his footsteps echoed from the room below, sending me courage. And then at last, when the hands on the clock pointed to ten and when it seemed that my labor would never end, the baby arrived.

As I lay in exquisite relief, Grace held the little one tenderly. "See," she said, "see the angel!"

The baby's wail brought John up the stairs. He came to me, arms outstretched, tears filling his eyes as he held me close.

"It's a girl!" Grace offered the baby for inspection. "And such a tiny one!"

For a moment, John looked at the squirming child. "Girl!" For nine months he'd thought of a boy and now he was confronted with a fragile girl of less than five pounds. Utter disbelief seemed his only reaction. He stared from the baby to me. As he gazed at the helpless little creature he began to smile. "A baby girl, Dolly! Did you hear that?"

Awed at first as Grace placed the baby crosswise on a pillow beside me, I studied the fuzz of hair, the miniature cheeks, the tiny snub nose, the swollen eyes. I felt the thin fingers, felt the soft pink feet. I pulled the pillow close. John leaned over her proudly, then kissed me again.

Grace noticed my questioning glance when she put a knit cap on the baby. "Her head is soft and must be kept warm. Keep it on for a month." I had never heard of a baby wearing a cap for a month, but I didn't say so. Nothing for her protection must be left undone!

I snuggled close to the baby. Through the window came the sound of the rushing river. I held her tighter, feeling the need to shield her.

John, too, was aware of the magnitude of our new responsibility. "She's so tiny. To hold her frightens me!"

Looking down, I recognized the cap on the baby's head. It was the one Mrs. Swen had given me.

Chapter 11

WORD SPREAD QUICKLY of the birth. Natives waited daily at the window for a glimpse of Mae, the first white baby born at Pilot Station. On the fourth day John carried me downstairs. I held the baby to the window. John uncovered the tiny feet, displayed the little fingers, laid the cap back for all to see. Gifts—tiny, beaded mooseskin bootees, rabbitskin mittens, wee mukluks, ivory dolls yellow with age and use—were shyly left at the door. With the care of a fragile baby an addition to our duties in the village, the days sped by. Every whimper and cry sent me scurrying to the baby's crib. At night, in an anxiety of wakefulness, it seemed to me that her breathing became too fast or too slow, her pulse raced madly or fluttered, she ate too little or whimpered too weakly. I remembered the Swens' baby, and, with new comprehension of our isolation, I felt a deepening anxiety in spite of myself. Apprehension was a giant striding in my wake. Then each morning brought reassurance and joy as I cuddled her eagerly.

When we heard of a dentist coming for a five-day stay at Marshall, the settlement forty miles away, we made plans for the journey. Our own acute need of dental care—a newly broken molar scraping my tongue, John's troublesome inlay—had to be weighed against the possible danger in taking a newborn baby on such a trip.

"So many ifs!" John looked toward the setting sun. "If the weather stays warm and dry, it could be an easy trip. But if the weather changes——"

Together we went to the window, gazing out at the darkening sky. . . .

The morning's sun was bright. Mae, snug in her own little bed, seemed to sense our preparations. Boxes of food and clothing, blankets and bedding, were carried to the launch.

Slowly the boat moved from its mooring. Pilot Station grew smaller. Steep cliffs rose and disappeared. Bowed branches, snags, gnarled trees and the tundra appeared on either bank. The baby stirred. The faintest breath of a change in the weather alerted us. The sky, overcast, a slight wind roughening the current, waves buffeting the flat-bottomed prow . . .

John stood at the wheel, listening to the growing wind. As the waves became whitecaps, the boat creaked and rolled.

The boat shuddered, and the motor's *chug-chug* strangled and coughed. John steadied himself. "Upriver, where it narrows, all hell will break lose." He stared anxiously at the baby as the boat wallowed alarmingly.

"Is there a shelter close?"

"God knows. I hope so!"

The baby cried, and I held her.

The waves rolled higher. The prow rose, shuddered and fell back. Dishes slid and clattered to the floor. I hugged the baby closer; fear, cold and clammy, crept up my spine and spread. I leaned over the baby, kissing the velvet cheek, cherishing her as I braced against the lurching boat.

John smiled at me. "I hope our teeth are worth it!" He relaxed slightly. Warmth and light and optimism flowed to me from him. "After this fling, maybe the weather will clear up."

I nodded. Already the heavens were clearing with the dying wind.

On our return from Marshall, letter writing was our first consideration. "Probably it'll be our last chance to send mail before the freeze," John said, finishing his toast.

"I've written all but the most important letters." I cleared the table and brought pen and paper. "We'll each write."

John looked at the sleeping baby. "How can we tell them———" He was thinking of how much we'd experienced together.

"She's the first grandchild. They'll want to know everything."

Mail arrived the next afternoon, and the letters sped on their way.

Watching John intent at his desk, I felt a warm glow of pride, and the present swung into focus. Being close to him made living a joy; and I felt no claims from the past in the letters we received. Clearly, our aloneness made each day ours, a pattern of warmth, of close communication, of a faith that nothing could destroy. Here, without others to intrude; here, without the world to demand our attention, we were content.

I turned from the sleeping baby to the pile of newly read letters. Tomorrow or the next day we'd unfold these pages and read them again.

September's chilly nights brought the first snow. Soon months would pass without the arrival of visitors.

"Listen to the dogs!" John exclaimed.

"It reminds me of last year—remember?"

From the window we watched the whirling flakes. "This year's isolation will make last year's seem anything but. Last year, Dolly, we had five white people to visit. This year, none." He reached down, twining his fingers in mine. "Do you think you can stand me for a year? It's a long time to hear only one voice."

"There'll only be two of us to do the work of seven. It'll be hardest for you, looking after the sick, butchering, keeping track of the herds. All that—plus inventories, ordering supplies for us, for the school and for the villagers. And records covering everything from counting wild fowl to recording weather information."

John grinned at that. "We'll do it, every bit of it!" The baby whimpered and he bent for her, cuddling her gently. He held the clenched, feebly thrashing fists. "This is the only job that would frighten me. The baby is your business."

"We've got so much to learn in the next few months."

We turned from the wintry scene to the schoolroom. The Eskimo children watched us while we planned the first day of school. We hoped to make up for our inexperience with understanding, labor and love. On Monday morning, John stepped outside and pulled the long rope attached to the bell high on the rooftop. The full throaty peal sounded over the whitening tundra to the village, echoing from the hill. Presently we saw them coming—fur-wrapped bodies bent against the chill; older children leading the little ones; the shy, the awkward, the timid; by twos and threes—they shuffled to the door of the school.

We helped them remove their parkas and guided them to the big oil-drum stove. As the children sat waiting for school to begin, we realized the stupendous job facing us. All grades and ages would be together. Some would understand no English; some would know only the simplest words. Notwithstanding, all must learn to read and write, and the older children would study history, geography and arithmetic.

John spoke to the children. I wondered how they would learn fractions, division and tables—how did one show them the meaning of such symbols? And maps with blue for oceans— how could they comprehend a map of the world when their world ended with the tundra and the great sweeping curve of the Yukon.

John left to me the task of setting this little world in order while he took up his other duties. Most of the children had been given English names by the missionaries who now and then passed through. Each surname was the father's first name; sometimes not, adding to the confusion of finding out who was who. Furthermore, many carried the names of persons who had died just prior to the children's birth, in the belief that the newborn was the spirit of the dead returning.

With John's help, my first task was to see that some of the children had baths. Little hands covered with grease and dirt were washed. John gave some of the boys haircuts; one or two at least had to be bathed. The process was a prolonged one, for water must be heated, then dumped into galvanized tubs. As soon as I finished the girls, John took over the bathing of the boys. Pursuing and stalking lice was our next chore. "The good book says to use kerosene," John said, flourishing a government manual, "so kerosene it will be!" With a small wad of cotton he dabbed every inch of scalp and every strand of hair with the diluted mixture. Soon the air was heavy with the odor of kerosene, but the children were free of lice.

But not for long: we discovered that the pests left eggs that hatched. And so the job began once more; day after day John battled new hordes, baffled that he couldn't conquer them. Then we realized that when the children left the schoolroom they returned to rooms and beds where the lice were incubating. It was no wonder our battle was a losing one.

The reindeer-skin beds must be full of lice. Outside their miserable huts the wind whistled; the children huddled under those skins for warmth. They couldn't give up such possessions, lice or no! Nor could we hope to clean the huts as they should be cleaned.

Nevertheless, every three or four weeks we turned once more to the kerosene.

Soon it was time for John and the men to direct the broad nose of the launch toward the slough that led to the reindeer camp. A cold blast warned of quickening winter. When the men returned, each family would receive its allotment of reindeer meat.

The gamy odor in our kitchen spread throughout the house. "Do you suppose we'll ever relish it?" I put a piece of reindeer meat on John's plate, a smaller piece on mine.

He ate with gusto. "Sure we will! Everyone else up here does." He saw my untouched portion. "Eat it, Dolly! After all, we're a long way from a butcher shop. Remember, we got so we liked evaporated potatoes and dried onions and dried eggs."

"I know." I faltered at the dark mouthful. "Next year maybe it'll taste better. But—in the meantime—how am I ever going to swallow it?"

Saturday was, as usual, our workday. Laundry must be scrubbed on the dented copper washboard; after the white clothes had been boiled, they must be hung outside or on improvised clotheslines in the schoolroom. Sundays I baked bread, rolls and other pastry. John split wood for the range and carried water from the spring above the house, filling the six buckets on the kitchen bench. Outside he cooked tubs of rice, bones and fish as food for the dog team.

As winter closed in, the men prepared for the final trip to the reindeer herds upriver.

During John's absence it would be up to me to see that classes were held as usual, the fires kept throughout the day and night, water carried from the creek and the dogs fed at their stakes.

On the morning they left there was no sun; the clouds hung heavy and dismal. Outside, the dogs hushed their yapping as the boat disappeared beyond the high bank, and soon even the echo of the motor drowned in the hush of a threatening storm.

I turned from the window and faced a room that suddenly seemed forlorn—the gray walls, the marred wainscoting, the ugly, roaring heater, the warped and mended chairs. I could go only to the window again and look to the river, the mountain.

At eight-thirty I had finished the chores. The baby slept. The fire roared. Diapers dried in the kitchen. I ran outside and pulled the bell rope, the resonant ding-dong sounding again and again. Perhaps John could hear it as the launch moved up the river. He would be thinking of home. We understood, John and I, that together we were proof against this lonely land; alone, each was as defenseless as a snowflake in the storm.

I turned from the bell to the children, touching their slight shoulders gently as their presence warmed the room. Singing and storytelling delighted them, for music and the land of make-believe was as dear to them as to children round the world.

Later we struggled with words and sentences. As often as possible, I used images referring to fishing and hunting to demonstrate meanings and numbers.

The day passed rapidly, and I was left to the evening and its chores.

After feeding the dogs, I locked up the sheds and went to the kitchen. I heated a can of stew and drank a cup of coffee, aware of the stillness, the plinking of a spoon. Each noise seemed so loud in the stillness that I dreaded to move in the squeaky chair. Finally, when baby Mae was asleep in her crib, I got ready for bed, comforted by her closeness as I sat reading old magazines John had discovered in the attic. Much, much later, when the oil lamp dimmed, I tucked the blankets more securely about her and crept under the covers, trying not to disturb the sleeping house. Outside, the night turned colder. New snow would be falling on the reindeer camp.

Chapter 12

THE RETURN OF THE MEN marked the approach of winter. A week after they pulled the launch to shore the river froze. In spite of the roaring stove and the protection of storm windows and doors we felt a certain helplessness as the snow closed in upon the village. Houses creaked all through the night, groaning under the weight of winter. Dogs howled in mournful disharmony. The winds buffeted fur-clad children as they struggled up the hill to school.

The river froze deeper, the eddies quiet under the encroaching sheaf of ice. Smoke belched from oil-drum heaters; women, sitting cross-legged near the stoves, chewed skins to soften them, made new parkas, mended others, using bone needles and sinew as thread. Men, bundled deep in furs, spliced dog harnesses which had been neglected during the summer of fishing. Over all the village settled the austerity of winter. No more would the paddle-wheel steamer signal of its coming or kayaks strain against the rushing water. This was winter, when only dog teams could be used on the Yukon trails, when no man ventured far alone except to heed the call for food, for help.

We too settled in our home for the deepening winter, while

the ice crept over the great river, stifling it. The gaping whirl-pools were closed and the current stilled; teams could safely cut new trails, sprint to winter fishing grounds near the opposite shore. The ptarmigan, donning his coat of white, moved without sound near the village.

John watched the hitching of the excited howling teams, the process of tying towline and sled to opposite stakes to keep the dogs under control and the lines from tangling; hitching the lead dog and team to the towline; then the quick release of the ropes at the moment of departure.

"Guess I'll try my luck today," he said.

He lined up the sled and tied it, pulled the towline straight and brought Kemoogan to his position as leader; as he led the other dogs to their positions, they reared and leaped and snapped in eagerness.

The slippery glinting hill led straight to the river. Below were dangerous hummocks, protruding boulders. He turned back to the dogs, excitement suffusing his face at the challenge of this new adventure.

"Jump in!" he begged. "It's our first chance for a ride alone!"

I backed away from the sled.

"We'll only be a minute."

In another instant I found myself sitting in the sled, clutching its sides tensely. The dogs, idle for so long, leaped and strained at the ropes. John leaned down. With a quick flick of the wrist he released the ropes.

It was a split second before Kemoogan felt himself free. With a tremendous lunge he moved to the top of the slope, the sled swerving and twisting and zigzagging in his wake. Not a sound squeezed past my lips.

I clung to the sled. Snow pelted my face; ice particles stung my cheeks. I closed my eyes and clung tighter.

Abruptly the dogs swung to one side and I was catapulted into the snow.

Bewildered at the impact, at the shooting pain in my arm, I sat holding my sleeve, waiting for John to dig me from the snow. He shook himself groggily and crawled to my side. As he helped me from the sled, I was still holding my arm.

"Dolly, are you hurt? Are you hurt, Dolly?"

All I could do was cradle the parka sleeve and wonder how one set a broken arm.

"Must have been that huge rock, Dolly. The brake struck it. Guess the sled flipped me and I came down on your arm. Here, let me see."

In our anxiety we forgot the dog team. The dogs were moving off, dragging the sled behind them. John raced, yelling, after it. Some of the villagers came running and shouting; some hooked up teams and sped after the dogs; John limped back to my side.

Together we plodded toward the house, John rubbing his tender hip.

"You sat down too hard," I said.

He winced. "Is your arm still broken?" He opened the door. "Here, I'll help you out of your parka."

We probed each other gingerly. His bruised hip was painfully swollen; my aching arm would soon be all right. As we stood there our eyes met. We began to laugh and could not stop.

"Amen!" John said finally, wiping his eyes. He went to the window. "And they've brought back our dogs. All's well."

After that, John often took the dogs on short runs to exercise them. When we were not busy with the school, he set snares for rabbits and ptarmigan, sank fishtraps under the ice and tracked fox.

As the days shortened and winter held us fast, we listened anxiously to Mae's increasingly fretful cries. Each night we stood beside her crib, shocked to see how frail she had become. We tried not to think of the little graves we had seen in Alaskan settlements. I'm not sure now whether John or I first thought of giving her sweetened condensed milk. I could only guess the amount, but we knew we must try everything. The fire blazed higher in the range, and soon the bottle was warm. At the touch of the nipple, the baby opened her mouth, swallowing in quick gulps. And as she did so, I backed to the chair, holding her close as she continued to feed.

Gradually she gained an ounce, two ounces; her cries lessened and we began to hope she would grow strong.

November's cold increased; with it came a sense of anticipation in the village. We saw the look on grizzled faces, among the women and the young as they trudged to the smokehouse or paused at the crest of the hill overlooking the frozen river. Or they talked at the water hole, kept free of ice, waiting and straining to hear something it would not have occurred to us to expect.

One day the villagers seemed to be in holiday mood. We saw them everywhere, going to the river. "What on earth—?" I began. Dogs howled, yanking at their chains, as a team appeared down the trail. We joined the waiting groups, not certain why we did. The team came closer and stopped. While the dogs lay panting in the snow, the driver of the team pointed down-river. Instantly feverish excitement gripped the crowd.

John stopped a child. "What's happening?"

"The eels come soon to our village. We catch them. We eat them and feed the dogs."

"They come up the river?"

"You see river? It rises fast. So many eels—they make the water rise. Every day we watch so we do not miss the eels."

Fascinated, hardly believing our eyes, we watched the river, the water creeping around the edges of the ice, the gigantic, inexorable push of the eel-run. But before the eels reached the village, it was time to call the children to school.

No one heeded the bell. Figures—old men, women, children—scurried everywhere, collecting nets, sticks, twigs and branches. From the door of the schoolroom we stared in wonder, not able to understand what they were about or why they needed sticks and branches. Wild yelling came from the river. One of the children was near, and John called to him. "What does it mean?"

The child beamed. "The eels are very close now."

Men, women and children armed with picks, nets, sticks, buckets, raced toward the river. Not far from the bank, the villagers broke holes in the ice. Suddenly there was another yell. We saw a fisherman hold up a small net writhing with eels. The river was so crowded with eels they might have been one of the elements.

Immediately the banks became a frenzied dipping, pouring, yelling mass of parkas. Hundreds of eels squirmed off nails, out of nets, off forked sticks and slithered to the ice at the catchers' feet.

No longer able to resist, John raced for his net and joined the yelling crowd. The eels were flung high on the bank where they froze almost at their first wriggling. Slowly the crowd moved upriver, following the flood of eels. Further and further the natives moved from the village; when at last the run ended, they began straggling home. Men hitched dog teams and went out to gather the frozen eels. Soon sleds were filled with eels to be brought back to the village and dumped beside the huts for use during the winter.

John piled his catch of eels beside our house. Frozen, ugly, they would be chopped up and fed to the dogs.

"Do the villagers eat them?" I asked.

"Sometimes they cook eels with rice. But usually they feed a small piece to each dog—only a small piece. Too much would be too rich a food." John tossed the last forkful onto the heap. "In a pot of rice, eel would make a good meal."

I grimaced, glad John did not suggest I cook eel in mushy rice.

He led Kemoogan to his stake. "I can understand now why the villagers look forward to the eel-run."

He pushed the parka hood back from his grinning face. "Quite a day! Feel as if I'd dipped eels all my life!" He looked toward the river. "Still hard to believe the size of such a migration. Just imagine how many hundreds of thousands of eels it takes to raise the level of the water at their coming."

"Where do they come from at this time of year?"

"The natives think that when the mud freezes at the shallow mouth of the river, the eels are forced into the open water in time for the harvest." He opened the shed door. "But why they come upriver, Lord knows; it's like manna from heaven in this country."

The excitement had hardly died when a reindeer, pulling a

sled, appeared on the far bank of the river, setting the dogs in such a frenzy that one tore from its chain and dashed across the ice after the deer.

John ran for his binoculars, sensing the trouble if the dog should attack and kill the animal. Panting like a thing gone wild, the dog raced toward the frightened reindeer. Suddenly the sled owner fired at the dog, the shot reverberating across the river.

"The dog's down. No, he's leaping at the deer——" John stopped, his mouth ajar; then he put down the binoculars. "The dog lived just long enough to hamstring the deer. They both went down."

That evening the men of the village gathered at the school, their faces reflecting the seriousness of the problem confronting them. John, with Burt as interpreter, explained they must decide who should pay damages. Did the deer-drawn sled have a right on the river? Whose fault was it that the dog had got loose? Did the deer owner have a right to shoot the dog?

Questions, gestures, ejaculations filled the tense room. The owner of the dog and the owner of the reindeer argued their rights. Each man presented his side to the jury. There were no lawyers. The court weighed the arguments and finally decided the deer owner must pay damages for shooting the dog. Without grumbling, the men left the room.

As John came out, Old Cyclone, one of the Eskimos, stood holding his swollen jaw, moaning with the agony of toothache. Saliva ran from his mouth and froze on the fur of his parka. John beckoned him to follow and opened the medicine closet.

"Old Cyclone again with a bad tooth," he explained, taking down a bottle. Dipping some cotton into the antiseptic he said to the man, "Open!" Gently John swabbed the tooth. Presently he patted the bent shoulder, nodding vehemently to show the pain soon would be over, then sent him home.

"Probably next week Old Cyclone will show us where the tooth used to be." John frowned as he eased out of mukluks. "Must take a lot of guts to pull your own tooth with a pair of pliers. But up here, when you know darned well you can't get help, you can do a lot of things you never thought you could."

Chapter 13

DECEMBER'S DUTIES left us rushed for time. Aside from the Christmas program, we must prepare a huge feast in the schoolroom. To an amateur cook it seemed as formidable and complicated as snuffing the Northern Lights—boiling a stew of rice and meat, baking pies, kneading bread, preparing coffee for every man, woman and child in the village and still teach school, rehearse the Christmas program and take care of all our regular duties!

"Just the two of us," I said to John. "How good a pastry maker are you?"

"We'll know soon enough."

But we couldn't disappoint the village, for Christmas was a tonic, a song lighting a somber world.

Together we began making dried-apple pies, and days were needed for this operation. As soon as one batch cooled it was frozen in the shed until the feast. In between batches we returned to our regular chores.

With the creek frozen, John carried water from the Yukon, each day cutting through new ice down to the water level. In midwinter the ice might be thirty or forty inches thick.

Breadmaking was next. Night after night we set the dough; by morning it was ready for kneading and shaping; by afternoon it was ready to be baked. Each batch was put with the frozen pies in the shed. The herculean task of cooking stew never ended. For hours kettles and more kettles of simmering deer meat were juggled back and forth on the range. A few canned carrots were added at the last, and then the whole dumped into dishpans. When all dishpans were used, we turned to the boiler and small washtubs. In time all batches were put out in shed with the thirty loaves of bread, the fifty pies.

During this rush we also practiced Christmas carols, the pantomime and simple dances with the children. On the last day, exhausted but excited by the spirit of Christmas, John and I sacked nuts and candy from our own supplies. These would be our gifts to our neighbors.

After decorating the tree in the schoolroom with colored paper chains, gleaming strips of tin snipped from cans and strings of popcorn, we dressed hurriedly. At the first shuffle of mukluks on the crust of snow outside we opened the door to a receptive, inspiring audience. Grinning, nodding, they greeted us and took seats. Simple good humor enlivened every face. Watching their kindliness, I was reminded that they were almost a single family, intermarrying within the village. No stranger was among them. And this night every child among them felt the pride of his elders as he rose to sing his song or speak the poem he had been taught.

Our glances roamed over the listening faces. There was Palmolive, who owned a large boat and traded furs for canned goods. He had developed an uncanny gift for such trading and knew which fox fur or mink would bring a good price. Near him sat Bill, who fished and hunted diligently. And there were others—

the poverty-stricken, the shiftless, the ill. Even the crippled had been carried to watch Amy, the orphan, recite her verse and Jim, the son of the trader, sing his song.

At the end of the program they grasped our hands, patted our backs, murmured "*Quiena, quiena*" again and again. Acknowledging their pleasure, we knew the weeks of toil had been worth while.

When the last visitor had gone, we went wearily to bed, stopping to listen to the baby's soft breathing as we leaned over her crib.

"Her new hair is blond," I whispered. "Isn't she a doll?" We smiled in the half-light at the snub nose, the black eyebrows and curling lashes.

"She's our whole world up here." John turned toward the bed.

"I know," I agreed, crawling under the blankets.

John lay staring at the ceiling. Finally he glanced at me.

"Dolly, there's one man here I'm not quite sure of—one I don't trust." He moved toward the edge of the bed and blew out the light. "Just to be on the safe side, I'm going to teach you to fire the gun. That should be fair warning to him."

I knew which of the villagers he meant—Joe, a half-breed, whose look had sometimes alarmed me. He seemed always to be watching me when I was outside alone.

John put his arm around me. Presently he spoke again. "It's nothing to worry about. Let's get some sleep."

We rose very early the next morning. The kitchen was crowded with the pans of bread, stew and dried-apple pies brought in from the shed to thaw. John hoisted the heavy pans to the range to heat while I got our breakfast. During breakfast we took turns stirring the stew-mash.

"Can't you dilute it?" John asked.

Buckets of water were heating for coffee, bread was crowded inside the oven to hurry its thawing. The pies were done. By eleven, families began arriving; some carried tin cups, some had spoons and birch bowls from which to eat.

John carried the pans of stew into the schoolroom where some of it was kept warm on the stove and asked the older girls to help serve, cut the pies and the bread. For a time only the rattling of spoons and cups rose above the noise of eating. There were seconds for all. John and I stood by, waiting for the tumult to subside before serving the Eskimo ice cream. Wild cranberries, salmon eggs and seal oil frozen. Even John wilted a bit at the prospect of enjoying it. "Want to try it?" he murmured wickedly, thrusting a spoonful under my nose.

"No—you take my share."

"Tomorrow." He grinned. "Maybe tomorrow, if I'm hungry then."

Some of our guests carried coveted leftovers in bulging kerchiefs, others took home what they could carry in heaped bowls and in cups. At last the final guests nodded their "*Quiena, quiena*," and closed the door, leaving the odor of parkas, of fish, stew and ravaged air behind them. John let a fresh blast of air inside the schoolroom, then together we went to enjoy the quiet of our home across the hall.

"What a day!" John said, collapsing in the rocker. "Christmas comes but once a year."

I sat beside him; my feet ached, my back felt the strain of hours of cooking. "Thank heaven for the vacation while you're at it," I said.

John leaned back, closing his eyes. "Remember last year—we had turkey and all the trimmings."

I nudged the mukluk from my foot. "And this year reindeer and fish."

"The important thing is that we're together this Christmas, you and I and our baby."

"I count our blessings, too, darling. It's not always easy to see them, I guess."

"But we're still going to have Christmas dinner! Tomorrow we'll go to the fishtrap, and if there's a salmon in it, we'll bake him."

The next morning, tucking Mae deep under blankets in the sled, and with the team yapping discordantly, we moved down the slippery embankment and skidded out to the river trail. Soon the sled found the pounded ruts of the main trail. The dogs settled down to a more leisurely gait, working well under Kobuk, an animal we were trying out as a replacement for Kemoogan's place as lead.

I watched Kobuk trotting rhythmically. He was gray and white, young and powerful. He had a mind of his own and he looked vicious and unfriendly. Often he growled as the whip sang over his head—a dog with spirit, intelligence and courage.

John yelled, "Haw," and the team veered to the left. The dogs moved toward the willow stakes marking the underwater fence of the fishtrap. They halted at John's command. Leaving the team, John cut the ice into a wide V where the sticks converged. Here, under the ice, would be the trap, filled, we hoped, with fish. Grunting with the effort of bringing the heavy trap out of the deep water, John spilled the salmon onto the ice. He whistled gleefully. "Not bad! Ten beauties! That takes care of our Christmas dinner."

As we returned to the sled, a harsh wind chilled us. Clouds darkened the sky in their quick scud across the heavens. A flock of white ptarmigan, huddled low as we approached, and soared overhead to light only a few yards away from the trail. Instantly John stopped the dogs and fired at the motionless flock. One ptarmigan was hit; the others flew away. John picked up the ptarmigan and tucked it in the sled at my feet. "Now you've two choices for dinner."

I kissed his cold, red cheek. "No pioneer could provide better," I said.

When we reached home, we found the mail had arrived. "End of a perfect day," John said. "We'll go again. Next time we'll go across the river and set snares for rabbit and ptarmigan."

After warming ourselves and the baby, we began the painful joy of opening letters—the first reactions to news of Mae's birth. We opened one letter and saved the rest to read after our Christmas dinner.

"If you'll clean the fish, I'll mix the dressing. . . ."

When dinner was ready, John held Mae, watching her eyes grow round in wonder at the sight of the candlelit tree. This was our first Christmas alone.

During the remainder of our vacation we worked and rested, went hunting and spent hours with Mae. And there were times when we had to care for the sick in the village.

But this was difficult, for then all came—the weak, the crippled, the tubercular. They came to our door, their eyes dull, their coughs resounding in the tiny room. And they came at any hour or followed us home. Often they spit into their cupped hands to show us how sick they were. They asked for aspirin, for chest plasters, for liniment. John visited the huts of those too ill to come. Often John was called on only after the medicine man had failed to cure them; often the medicine man returned when John had gone and took away the pills or tablets, giving the patient willow bark to chew. When a villager died, the body, dressed in a parka, would be placed in the yard, crossed stakes at head and feet to hold the body off the ground, and lie frozen throughout the winter. In the spring, when the thaw softened the earth, a grave would be dug for the body, or for what remained of it. If we had not insisted on burial, the body would have been left to rot or be eaten by dogs or wolves, for the Eskimos believed that the spirit of the dead had already returned to the village in the birth of a new child. Sometimes, we heard, the body would be abandoned on the tundra, to help the spirit of the dead more easily escape.

In winter the huts were sealed tight. The increase in tuberculosis seemed inevitable. In school we attempted to teach hygiene, explaining the danger of sharing the utensils of those who were ill; the prospect of contagion when the mother prechewed the food she gave to her baby; how epidemics spread as the result of careless spitting and coughing. But those who listened to our warnings were usually those who were the least in need of our efforts to help. At times, in a mood of helplessness, we roamed far from the piteous cries, escaping from the prospect of disaster in search for the serenity needed to continue what seemed an impossible task. We headed upriver for the fishtraps and the snares.

Finding the snares was often a chore in itself, for new snow hid them. Tracks told us where to look. We watched for the three-toed track of the ptarmigan leading to the hanging noose, and John's willow stakes. We hunted for snowshoe tracks. Now and then John pointed out a fox hunching low and escaping with the prey from one of our traps.

When the day ended, we had to return to the village and the sick who were waiting for us. John knelt beside the deerskin bed of ailing Ba Man, one of the old men. When the sick man raised himself weakly, John gave him a drink, holding his flesh-less neck, smiling into the sunken eyes, humble and helpless at the closeness of death. Outside, the old man's son gathered an-other armload of wood for the three generations within these somber walls. John turned to the door. Three generations! All drinking from the same rusted enamel dipper dangling over the water bucket, dipping fingers into the same battered kettle of fish. When the paroxysm ended, Ba Man fell back exhausted. Lying there, white, facial bones protruding, breathing shal-lowly, his chest seeming scarcely to move, his skeletonlike arms too weak to support his gnarled hands, he was the symbol of all his people, struggling to live against all prospect of hope.

As we returned home, the image of Ba Man lingered. We could not enjoy our own good health.

"If only we could do something!" John said bitterly. It was a question we often asked—yet not a question: an outcry against death, against our own frailty.

"We do what we can, John. Perhaps we can help a few a year!"

A few a year! Already waiting burial in the spring were the frozen bodies of a man, a woman and a baby. Tomorrow, perhaps, there would be the body of Ba Man, a reminder of the helplessness of all those who came to Alaska to teach, to guide and to protect!

"Every death leaves me shocked as if our own child had died. I can't take them medicine and food and not feel how much they expect of us. They're not strangers to me, even in these few months. I see it when I open the door. And all I can take them is aspirin and liniment."

John got up and put on his parka; it was time to feed the dogs. It was clearer, this trip north. Remembering our decision to stay another year, to undertake the care of a village—we had a need to give a part of our lives.

Chapter 14

IN FEBRUARY accidents and sickness plagued the village. John, returning from the fishtraps, heard a desperate call from a sled: "Come quick! Dog team jump little boy. Tear his neck deep, like this!" The driver of the sled clawed at his neck to show us.

John grabbed gauze, bandages and antiseptics and stumbled down the bank toward the other team. Evening was falling before he returned. Blood splattered his face, caked his hands and stained his boots. His eyes were still stunned with what he'd seen. I waited, watching him pour water from the teakettle to the washbasin and soap and scrub the dried blood from his hands before changing clothes.

Presently only the whiteness of his face told the story of grim, bitter hours. He stooped over the baby, feeling her forehead.

"Still feverish." He nestled her in his arms.

"I'll get you something to eat."

"No," he said. "Don't bother. Not now. I'm not hungry." And he kept on rocking Mae.

After a time I brought him a cup of strong, black coffee. "The boy died," I said.

"We were too late. He'd bled too much."

"Who was it?"

"A little fellow from another village. Ran out to meet his father. The dogs jumped him before his father could stop them. The dogs ripped his chest and neck, clear to the jugular vein."

I looked at John's hands. I took the sleeping baby from him and put her on the couch. He didn't notice. "There wasn't a thing—not a thing—I could do."

Only concern for Mae helped John forget so terrible a death. Her fever was not high, but she was feverish. Before we could decide what to do, another dog team arrived. The driver called our names; the voice was familiar. I put on a fresh pot of coffee and hurried more food.

When the visitor entered, I stood at a loss. It was——Mr. Bowen. We had met him and his wife on board the *Boxer* on our way to Alaska. It was not so much the warmth of the fire that brightened the house that evening but the warmth of friendship and understanding, of contact with someone other than the hungry, the destitute, the ailing.

The baby was awake now, and Mr. Bowen noticed her flushed face at once and smiled. "The way she's drooling and biting her fists—she must be teething!"

We grinned foolishly and with great relief. Surrounded by the sick, we had not considered that Mae's fever might be a normal part of her development.

The following day, with Mr. Bowen's help, John visited all the sick. "What about Eluck's baby?" I asked anxiously when they got back.

"It arrived . . ." And John told how they'd found Eluck, in blinding pain, squatting on the floor of her hut, her feet spread far apart, her face buried in her hands. The men stood in mute compassion as she screamed.

"This way, baby come faster," the midwife explained.

"The baby has been given the name of Ba Man," John said.

A few days after Mr. Bowen's departure, John decided to make a trip to Marshall to sell our dog Kemoogan.

"The trail's hard. The weather's perfect. The fresh air and the trip will be good for us all!"

"Tomorrow's Saturday," I replied. "Let's go if the weather looks nice."

The day dawned bright. Moments after Mae and I settled ourselves on the sled, we went zooming onto the river. I smiled up at John's hooded face. The enchantment was all about us: the panting dogs stringing in easy rhythm, the baby deep beneath her skins cooing with the peaceful rocking. Everywhere the living seemed to be sleeping. I listened to the zing of the whip far over Kemoogan's head; I heard Kobuk's soft growl. The trail left the main river and cut over a high ridge. The steep pitch sent the sled hurtling after the dogs and left me gasping. Then the trail spanned what must have been a small lake and once more cut into the main river.

The dogs slowed down, and John, still guiding the sled, ran between the runners to relieve the sled of his weight. I handed him a pilot cracker and nibbled one myself.

In late afternoon we saw the settlement of Marshall and heard the village dogs. The trader's wife, Tilly, greeted us, taking Mae in her arms, opening wide her home where the coffeepot, fresh bread and cookies waited. Tilly cuddled Mae against her bosom, humming a tune that none but Mae could hear. Mae took her bottle snuggled against the warm breast.

For hours we talked, drank coffee and ate cinnamon rolls and sugared doughnuts.

In the morning John's throat was sore. "Feels like the flu," he said. But this was the day we were to leave for home, and John insisted that we go in spite of his fever.

He got groggily out of bed. "No, I'll be all right. I'll sell Kemoogan and we'll head for home."

He began dressing resolutely. "I might be sick a week. No, we can't stay. But you'll have to drive the sled."

I'd never attempted to take the dogs out before. John could see how nervous the idea made me. "You can do it. Kobuk is a good leader."

"But, John, he's never had to take orders from me."

In wretched silence I imagined myself clinging to the back of the sled. Ahead moved the dogs, sensing my uneasiness, listening for their master's word; my throat was dry, wordless; the dogs turned, sniffing, tangling in their harness, fighting to the death. . . . Or the sled would overbalance on a step bank and roll over; or Kobuk, a one-man dog, would refuse to obey; or he'd take the trail that swung upriver or toward the deer camps or toward the traplines and fishtraps. How would I know until too late? I began to wish we'd never left home.

John laughed at my protests. "I'll be there to help, darling. Don't worry so much about it."

"I know. Why did it have to happen this week end of all week ends?"

We made up the feather bed and went downstairs. John could not eat. Jim and Tilly gave him quinine and aspirin, but he shivered alarmingly.

"You'd best stay here," Tilly said, cuddling the baby. "Flu is nothin' to fiddle with."

"Plenty of room," Jim said, "and Tilly would be right glad to have this youngun for a while."

But John shook his head. "If you'll just take Kemoogan, we'll be on our way."

I looked out at the restless dogs and sank back into my chair. Kobuk always frightened me; his eyes seemed so cold, and often I'd seen him watching John at the fishtraps, eyes wicked in their coldness.

I couldn't look again at the yapping, straining dogs. While John and Jim went to hook up the team, I gathered our belongings and slipped the parka over my head. Tilly sacked some of her doughnuts and rolls.

"They'll come in right handy tonight," she said.

John's whistle summoned me. I clung a moment to Tilly's rough hands and kissed her. "Thanks for everything . . ." She slipped her arm around me. As John's whistle came again, she kissed Mae's cheek. For a moment she hid her face in the depths of the blue blanket, and I knew she was thinking of her own child who had died. "Take good care of her," Tilly said.

I moved slowly down the steps toward the sled, holding our precious baby. I turned once more and waved, a tear freezing to my cheek.

John waved me into the sled. "I'll start the team and see that Kobuk gets on the trail."

As if feeling his new responsibility, Kobuk immediately bent to the lead-lines. When the trail wound far ahead without a break, John stopped the team and had me take his place.

"It's all yours, Dolly!" His eyes were bloodshot and his lips blue. "Can you manage?"

I put my foot hard on the brake and clutched with shaking hands the rounded back of the sled. John settled himself, holding Mae beneath the furs.

"Mush!" I yelled. The strength and courage of my voice startled and shocked me as it echoed over Kobuk's head, sending him racing on the trail. Still clinging fearfully to the sled, I looked down at John and Mae huddled beneath the skins. In that moment I felt the challenge as Kobuk did. I watched for the high banks and the low ones that signified the changing course of the river. Kobuk kept his line straight, trotting with a rhythmic up-and-down motion from his head to his rump, looking back at times as if for encouragement on this, his first trial. Kobuk seemed to sense the need for hurry, his master's illness, and to miss the voice he'd grown to trust. He leaned into the harness as the sled topped a small hill.

At the steep bank skirting the frozen lake I helped push the weight of the sled over. Then we hurtled down the opposite side, sending the sled pressing at the dogs' heels. On the river ice I glanced at the sky darkening with storm clouds. We fairly flew over the slick trail.

The shadowy sky darkened. Darkness settled on the horizon. Still Kobuk pulled steadily on. Suddenly the dogs strained harder. Faintly, far ahead, came the faint howl of dogs chained in the village.

Kobuk swung to the right. John sat up, looking around dazedly. And there we were.

Chapter 15

MARCH BROUGHT the first breath of spring, a breath so soft one could scarcely see its coming. Snow still fell on old snowdrifts; ice still crunched beneath our feet; the river looked as solid and unyielding as it had in January. Yet the earth's promise hovered near. The young sun shed a warmer ray on immense icicles; bushes stirred, black stalks glistening. And the children began to stay longer out of doors. Even Mae, holding tight to the cushions, walked proudly the length of the couch. When, toward the end of the month, the older children were late or missed school entirely, we went to Grace for explanations.

"They go to the *cajim*," she told us. "They practice for the native dance."

We'd never been inside the lodge but had seen its half-buried roof. "Would they let us come to watch their dances?" John asked.

She nodded. "It is next week."

A week later we were invited to visit the underground *cajim.* "Stoop!" John held aside the reindeer skin covering the first

161

entrance. The passage was very small; we had to enter on hands and knees. We paused in the dimness, overwhelmed by the conglomeration of odors and noise.

As we grew accustomed to the interior of the hut, we saw squatting figures all about us. On the ground sat the women; directly above them on narrow ledges perched the men and boys. Confused at the din of drums and the animated dancers, we tried to get our bearings. I didn't know whether I should squat with the women or stay with John.

Reaching for my hand, John moved along the wall, hunting for a place where we could sit. He hoisted me to the ledge. The great skin drums thudded and thumped.

Two men sat astride a log, facing each other and stripped to the waist, feathered headdresses cascading down their backs. Weaving back and forth on the log, chanting the story of a seal hunt, the men acted out the adventure for the listeners. Perspiration glinted on their naked shoulders as they reached the climax of their story. The drums became louder, more insistent. The air about us throbbed with the wild rhythm.

Four women stood in a semicircle behind the men in the pit, rocking gently, whirling above their heads wands or switches from which tufts of feathers dangled. The feather wands dipped and bowed and reached and swirled, weaving an enchanting curtain in the shadows, holding us spellbound.

Drums throbbed; the chanting reached a crescendo that shook the *cajim*; then the drums were silent, the men relaxed, the feathery wands drooped. The audience rested a moment before another tale began.

This time they described the hunting of a polar bear. The wands performed the dance and the drum kept time.

When the dancing ended, we slipped from the ledge. The

crowd separated into chattering groups. After one last look we crouched and crept through the reindeer skin opening.

The sod roof of the *cajim* was behind us. We breathed deeply and looked up at the stars.

The thought of home grew stronger every day.

"It'll soon be time for geese and ducks again," John said, bringing in wood for the night. "And the thaw."

I snuggled Mae in her blanket. "And after that—home!"

John looked up from the crackling fire. "You're homesick!" Closing the stove door, he reached for my hand. "Are you?"

I smoothed Mae's blanket. "It's only that we'll soon be going. After all, it's been two years. And no one has seen the baby."

"And we've got money saved so we can go back to college for more training."

"Then you really want to go back?" I asked eagerly.

John said, "We've done our share. And think of all we've learned!" He grinned.

I crept into bed. The evenings were longer; already the day went to bed late, twilight lingering. I lay unable to sleep, my mind filled with thoughts of home.

Spring was coming. And with it the break-up, the opening of the river to the world outside. No more bitter winds or blizzards; no longer exiled from medical care and from those we loved.

I thought of all John had done—caring for the sick, teaching, keeping records. And the courage he had given me. And his patience in handling village disputes.

I rolled over. Twilight had gone, and darkness was settling over the baby's box bed, the oak chair. Soon the moon would rise.

The days lengthened and the snow melted. The villagers prepared for spring camp; ducks and geese wheeled overhead. In the midst of this expectant stirring, school drew to a close. When at last each little desk was cleared of its clutter, I stood at the door of the schoolroom, watching the children go.

John came along to tell me the mail was arriving. "Looks as if the ice were buckling a bit through the middle. The river must be coming up pretty fast."

"We must send back word that we'll be leaving in June," I said. "They'll be anxious."

I waited for John to agree.

He bit a piece of toothpick. "I don't know why, but I wish the mail team wasn't coming today."

When the dogs climbed the hill, we rushed toward the sled. In a moment we'd have the joy of hearing from home. While John helped the driver sort our mail, I picked up Mae. Soon we would be leaving and she'd see Grandma and Grandpa! I touched her pale cheek and her thin hands. Then the door closed, and John and I began to read our letters. I saw John's face alter. My hands began to shake.

"John——"

He looked up, his face gone gray. "Dolly—our investment—it's all gone. We haven't any money left." He handed me the letter. "The mill's gone broke."

I was unable to trust my voice as the past months swept before my eyes. Suddenly, at the prospect of having to stay longer, I buried my face in my hands.

John was talking as if to himself. "If we leave now, we're broke—dead broke! Not even a cent saved."

I recognized his despair.

"Two years, Dolly! Now what?" And I couldn't answer.

"You could go home," John said finally. "I could stay another year."

I shook my head. I got up and wandered to the kitchen. I put the coffeepot on and set cups in front of us.

"I don't care for myself," John said, "but for you and Mae . . ."

I felt for his hand. "We've been lucky, but———"

"You go home, at least for the summer."

"Only if you go too! Why can't we both go, John? John—please. Then in September we'll come back again for another year!"

"The Indian Bureau would object."

"It won't do any harm to ask! Please, John—send them a telegram and see what they say!"

Some of the darkness left his face. "If we did get permission, I wonder if we could catch a boat?"

I put my arms about his neck. "We'll be ready! I bet we can make it!"

He pulled me to his lap. "Let's hope so." He picked up the letters. "Here, let's finish the mail . . ."

The water rose deeper along the frozen banks. Bigger streams, awakening now, sent water spilling into the current. The river ice heaved and buckled. Dog teams moved cautiously over the honeycomb of ice.

Magnificent flights of fowl, wheeling overhead, challenged John's skill. Returning at dusk with his game bag full, he was filled with awe at the canopy of beating wings which darkened the sky. Each day we waited for news from the Indian Bureau. The possibility of our leaving for the summer was always in our thoughts. At other times we made elaborate plans for the summer's work, certain we would not be allowed to go.

"We'll take the baby across the river to the berry patches," John said one day. "She must see everything."

"We'll have to take care she doesn't get eaten alive by the mosquitoes."

"It'll be fun, just the two of us showing her all that's to be seen."

The two of us . . . Just the two of us and Mae.

I pushed more wood into the stove and tried not to think of home.

In May the sun rose earlier, warming our world. The icicles hanging from the eaves dripped steadily; snowdrifts softened into eroded blankets; the river ice was covered with a film of water. We waited for the cracking, the splintering that would signal the break-up of the ice. Would we hear of a waiting ship, or would a note refusing us a vacation arrive from the Indian Bureau?

I hurried washing, mended and ironed our summer clothing. "Baby has so little," I said. "Her dresses are too small, and she has nothing for her feet except the beaded mooseskin bootees Grace made her. And no coat."

"The things you ordered ought to be on the first boat."

"If we're lucky. Even our clothes are shabby beyond words."

Danger threatened the villagers in the lowland as the river rose. There was a fear that the water might catch some of them. There was a rumor of an old woman left to die, of children abandoned, of dogs tethered and whimpering at their stakes. John organized a search party to make sure everyone had fled to higher ground. John knew the break-up might begin at any moment, but he had to take the chance.

I sat for hours at the window, watching the frozen river,

waiting for John to return. I kept seeing the men in kayaks creeping along the river's edge, trusting their flimsy boats, stopping now and then to listen for a cry for help. I slumped in a chair, trying not to think of the kayaks caught in an advance of thundering water and hurled against the rocks. Wretched, I wandered about the kitchen, listening for the first roar that would mean death to all who rode the river or attempted to cross the ice in sleds.

I forced myself back to my mending; I searched for more clothes to mend; I packed and cleaned and scrubbed.

At midnight a message came from John. He was safe—or had been safe when he sent someone to reassure me.

At two in the morning I pushed wood into the stove and made more coffee. At three I drank a final cup and at four I heard John at the door.

He smiled faintly as he took off his Mackinaw. "They're safe. All safe."

Two days later a deep reverberation thundered across the sweep of land at Pilot Station. The whole earth convulsed, crumbling the riverbanks, as the mass of ice started its violent journey to the sea. Trees quivered and were wrenched from the frozen earth. A large fishing boat shuddered as a giant block of ice rose behind it. The mass towered above the vessel, then plunged downward, bearing the splintered hull with it. We stood speechless and in awe at this display of power. Here, men were helpless. Here, men stood in the presence of inexorable force, all the more terrifying because it could be anticipated but not controlled.

The ice jammed, and the river rose above the banks, coming close to the steps leading to our yard. We measured the distance to the house; if necessary, we could retreat to the hill.

A few more feet would bring the river into the yard; a few

more feet and our launch would be crushed like the fishing boat. In the village, water would be closing in on some of the native huts. Soon they would be wrested from their flimsy foundations. Already some of the villagers were scrambling up the steep hill, babies strapped to their backs, kerchiefs full of dried fish. More trees trembled, swayed and disappeared into the river. The villagers gathered quietly on high ground. Rowboats, staked on the shore, swung and grabbed at their ropes and were crushed or taken by the river. A kayak was plucked from its mooring. We saw it snap in two, as if broken in the jaws of a whale.

John put his hand to my shoulder. Mae whimpered and I held her close without taking my eyes from the river. Dinnertime had come and gone. Reluctantly I hurried inside. While the venison steak cooked and the vegetables steamed, I kept watch at the window. Suddenly the little group outside shifted. Almost as one, the little group broke up and started across the footbridge toward their homes. The ice had broken free again; the danger of flood had passed. Now, for the moment, they were safe.

When John came in for dinner, the water had stopped only a few feet away from the house; ice flowed as far as we could see. Yet now we could relax, for the river was dropping as swiftly as it had risen. Below us the ice jam had broken.

Throughout the night the village men took turns on watch, but by morning the ice pack still flowed toward the sea.

Gradually the ice thinned; patches of river broke through in giant swirling whirlpools. Lone chunks of ice floated in the main current; later came logs and trees from upriver. Wood for building, wood for fuel. The men jumped into kayaks to catch the best of it.

John watched, then he too paddled out in a kayak, for wood

was always scarce. At first he ventured only close to the shore; then, farther out into the current, he spotted a beautiful pole and paddled furiously to catch it before the river flung it from him.

Suddenly the men at my side began to call to him. Farther and farther he went, and louder called the men, waving to him frantically. As I watched, I felt he could never hear them in the roar of the river, but I joined my voice to theirs in an attempt to attract his attention.

Suddenly he turned about; he saw the waving arms, sensed our frantic warning, then tried to escape the swirling current just ahead of him. In that instant, a whirlpool clutched the pole, flung it high and swallowed it . . . down . . . down.

At that moment John seemed to recognize the perils; like a man fighting an overwhelming avalanche of water, he bent to the paddle, crouching, straining, pulling with all his might as he felt the spreading backwash.

Two of the village men jumped in their kayaks and began fighting toward him. I watched the others sweep closer and closer to him in their flimsy boats. Now and then they rested; now and then I heard them shout. Finally I knew he had won. I hid my face, unable to keep back the sobs of fear and relief.

We stumbled toward each other, and the villagers fell silent and abruptly turned up the bank toward their stained, dark huts, looking back at John, who still staggered from his ordeal and the weight of water in his soaking Mackinaw.

We continued to wait for permission to return to the States.

"The *Victoria* will be leaving Seattle. We won't be able to make it unless word comes through right away."

"Everything's ready," I reminded him. "What if, once we get there, we decide to stay?"

"But we can't, Dolly. We've already promised to come back for another year."

"If we leave everything behind us, we'll just have to come back."

John said, "If we could only see our way clear to stay. If things had turned out as we'd planned, it wouldn't make any difference." He led the way up the stairway to bed. "It won't be so bad to stay another year if we can have the summer with our families." He brought the covers up to his chin. "I don't mind for myself, but for you and the baby. It's a tough life for a woman, being shut indoors month after month." He waited for me. "I suppose it's a lonely life without other women for company. For men, Alaska's a paradise of hunting and trapping, excitement and adventure with the dogs, the boats." He rolled toward me. "I wonder if you know what I mean when I say that this life grows on a man—no pressures, no worries, none of the hurry and tension and competition in a world ready to gobble up a man who doesn't fit the pattern."

I said, "You'd always want to live like this?"

"No, not exactly."

We lay thinking back over the two years. Life in some ways had been so full, so rewarding, but there were some intangibles we lacked and greatly missed—our families, our friends, the familiar things Alaska did not have to offer.

John's permit to leave reached us the following Monday. Since the *Victoria* had already sailed from Seattle, we got Grace's husband to take us down the Yukon to St. Michael to reach the boat. The next two days were sleepless; in our haste last minute chores seemed never to be done.

Then miraculously we were aboard the launch, and far out from shore the *Victoria* stood waiting.

Chapter 16

Traveling toward the big ship now, I remembered John's words about the new kind of shyness we would feel. On board we went directly to our stateroom. At dinner I suddenly realized that our mended clothes were out of date, and the feeling that the world had swept past us made me uneasy. This was a strange, annoying feeling, difficult to cope with; there was no way I could ease my mind. My first thought was to creep away and hide myself, but this I could not do.

"What does it matter?" John said. And he was right, for the curious gazes weren't unkind. They were interested in us and in the life we'd been leading in the wilds.

On the second day a sea of glittering ice faced us, hemming the *Victoria* in a world of whiteness, slowing us so the ship seemed hardly to advance. Now and then the ship moved gently, testing the barricade.

Excitement touched us as a spectacular snowstorm touches the hearts of little children. We watched the field of ice jostle all around us. And when at last the green sea opened, we breathed a sigh of relief not unmixed with a sense of loss that a time we would remember had ended.

Early in July we saw the Seattle waterfront. As the ship docked, we saw John's parents waiting. The swift taxi ride startled us; the noise of trains, horns, streetcars and busses frightened Mae. There was no comforting her in this world of confusion.

The next day, after borrowing a car, we started the drive to my home. It was warm. Haze settled in the valleys as mile after mile slipped by. Gradually silence settled in the old car; the baby, nervous at this world she'd been so ruthlessly introduced to, fretted and slept. John's hands, unaccustomed to steering a car over rough roads, tensed and gripped the wheel.

Nothing had changed, yet the whole world had changed since our going. The fields were ripening. It was all the same. I settled back, remembering—the wild, sweet strawberries down the lane, the tiny blackberries on the hillsides, the huckleberries high in the mountains.

John put his hand on my arm. "Recognize where we are?" The great trees where the tire swing hung, the red barn just a curve away ... and suddenly the house was there with its wide porch, the pump, the roses tied securely against the wind. This was the home I'd dreamed about; here was the serenity I missed.

John turned into the drive and honked the horn. And then I saw my mother at the kitchen door and my father behind her. For a long moment I couldn't move.

As soon as we could control our voices we turned to the baby. She was on her knees in the car, watching us through the window, her large blue eyes wide.

John carried Mae to the house. On a table lay gifts—her first real shoes, bonnets, beautiful clothes. We slipped off the mooseskin bootees and dressed her in her finery, but the "ohs" and "ahs" frightened her and we waited before slipping on the dainty pink **dress.**

It was my father who first raised the question of our plan to return to Alaska. The warm kitchen was quiet. John's fork scraped his plate.

I couldn't meet my father's eyes, but I could feel them. He pushed back his chair. Mother said nothing. In the face of their disappointment, our reasons for returning to Alaska seemed unimportant, insignificant.

"But money's as easily made here," my father said.

I raised the coffee cup to my lips, for his words reminded me of my homesickness at Pilot Station, in a land so bare that even he could not imagine how forlorn it was. But still, for just one last year . . .

"We've left everything we own behind us."

Mother said, "We've taught you never to lament the loss of things you can buy. The important thing is, all three of you are safely home."

John turned to me. He was thinking of the river, the ice and the blizzards; of the sick and the poor in their helplessness. All these came back to John as they did to me.

We couldn't change our plans.

Reluctantly my parents accepted the decision, and for the remainder of the summer John and I were free to roam the banks of winding creeks, hike and stroll, drinking in the fullness of these hours, blotting out the sudden memory of mosquitoes and raging rivers and lonely trails; forcing ourselves to forget how soon we would be going as we greeted old college friends, such as Stan and Ethel Gray.

Only after many questions did we realize that Stan's interest in Alaska was more than casual.

"Yes," Ethel said breathlessly, "just the two of us. A honeymoon like yours."

Stan crossed his legs. "In fact it's about settled."

Ethel turned to me. "Mother and Dad tell us it isn't safe. If anything happened—but what could happen? We're both healthy, and Stan—why, just look at Stan!"

"Have you applied for jobs?" I asked Ethel. I tried to imagine the effect of the pale blue sweater, the flawless skirt, the expensive shoes on the Eskimos at Pilot Station.

"It's to be some place north of the Bering Sea, on some river—can't remember the name now!"

Watching her small, dainty face, I felt suddenly the cold of piercing winds, the sting of freezing air. All the worries, fear, and oppression of isolation swept the bright sun into dullness; for a moment this blithe girl sat on a desolate riverbank, bewildered by the premonitions that stalk the uneasy mind. I looked at Stan. But the river has no regard for a man's strength. Nor does the blizzard that swoops across the tundra or the whirlpools that lie beneath the weakening ice.

"We couldn't wait to tell you!" Ethel said.

"It's a wonderful place for hunting and fishing," John exclaimed. "Talk about ducks and geese! But it's a rugged country, believe me! I wish we could be closer to where you'll be."

Stan was without fear. "Nothing's going to happen."

John hesitated. "I want to be honest with you, Stan. I can't possibly tell you what you're letting yourself in for. If you go fishing and don't come back, if you go hunting and don't return —well, who's going to look after Ethel? She can't call her folks or a doctor—she can't even leave!"

I felt I had to warn Ethel. "Do you know how to have a baby alone? Can you tend the sick? You'll see bodies so emaciated that only the spirit seems to live; you'll see the dead, frozen. . . ." I faltered, watching a bee cradle itself in a lily.

"But it might not be like that at our station," Stan said in hope and ignorance. "Besides, we expect it to be exciting. That's why we're going."

Remembering his own enthusiasm, John smiled. "Just watch your step, Stan!"

As they left, John and I watched them go. "They didn't hear a word we said."

The days went more rapidly as September approached—family picnics, trips to the beach. At last, the day for good-bys, the moment I'd dreaded, the last walk around the old home. And then the car moving, the gate swinging shut.

We had arranged to return by the overland route; a ship to Seward, from Seward by rail. The sea voyage aboard the larger boat was much more comfortable than our earlier voyages. Panorama after panorama spread before us. Mountains towered in greens and purples.

On deck Mae, dressed warmly against the wind, toddled beside us with her doll. John grinned in deepest pride at the tiny figure.

"You'd hardly recognize her," he said tenderly. "Little shoes instead of moccasins." He swung Mae to his shoulders. "There's Seward, straight ahead."

For some passengers Seward meant the end of a journey; for others, for us, for Elva Stephens and Helen Mayo, it meant little more than half of the distance to go.

Chapter 17

As THE TRAIN PULLED out of Seward, Elva sat ahead of us, her little daughter nestling against her. Helen seemed preoccupied. I shook my head at John's questioning look. "Homesick, very likely."

The engine pulled us past majestic hills, over ravines so vast they sank from sight, over chasms which made me hold my breath.

Pausing briefly at Mt. McKinley, racing through Matanuska Valley, sleeping at the Curry Hotel, we pushed farther north, coming closer to the wilderness we'd left so easily in June. Now and then John's arms tightened around Mae, and I understood his mood. Now that we'd abandoned security, his confidence in his judgment was wavering.

"Mae is a year old now," I said, "and the winter should be easier."

Elva interrupted to ask about what lay ahead for her. John asked the age of her daughter. "It'll be a lonely winter," he said, "with just the two of you."

When John was elsewhere, Elva told me of her husband, their quarrels, the separation, the attempt to avoid divorce. Her voice broke, leaving only the creaking and swaying of the train.

I hunted for words. "You have your child——"

She rose abruptly as Helen joined us. Dark, petite, the antithesis of a pioneer, Helen tweaked one of Mae's curls. "You must have exciting times up here."

I nodded. "We've seen and visited places we'll never see again. We made friends and saw them leave and felt bad that miles or a lifetime would separate us." Council . . . Ophir Creek . . .

"Our dog teams——" I paused. I was aware that I hadn't answered Helen's question. "You'll understand later what I mean. Are you planning to stay a year?"

"I only wish I knew! Alaska has always seemed challenging, but all this distance from a city—do you think I'll miss city life?"

"You've never been away from a city?"

Blithely she shook her head. She gave me a long look. "You make me begin to doubt my decision." She frowned at the rushing landscape.

At John's return she appealed to him. "At least you folks won't be too many miles away in case I need help!"

John, trading glances with me, nodded. "That's right. A two-day trip by dog team."

She looked wretched. "Two days!" She faltered. "You mean —you couldn't possibly get there——"

"It would be a wonder if we did."

Stunned, she looked at Mae. "But what did you do when you had your baby?"

"What did we do? We prayed."

She would learn, as we did.

Nenana, where we were to leave the train, was just ahead. Elva and Helen showed their bewilderment. "How do we go on from here?"

"There's a boat to take us to the Yukon," John said.

Nenana looked a gaunt outpost of civilization. There were fishing shacks at the water's edge. Moments later John and I entered the old hotel. Elva and Helen were staying somewhere else. As we went to bed at last, someone knocked at the door. We heard Helen's shrill voice. John let her in. "What's wrong?" he asked.

"Elva. Something's happened—something dreadful! Look at my hands!"

John went to help if he could. When he came back I knew what had happened to Elva. John sank to the chair. "She was hemorrhaging, bleeding worse than you can imagine."

"But——" I remembered Elva's bitter story of an attempted reconciliation with her husband.

"I know one thing. She's lucky to be alive!" He got in beside me and put his hands behind his head. "She kept calling for her husband."

"She can't go on," I said. "She'll have to wait until she's stronger and then go home."

The next morning we went over to see Elva. "It was a jolt for Helen," John said as we climbed the stair. "She was white as a sheet." He knocked at the door. "Don't look shocked."

But my heart sank as I saw Elva's head move weakly on the pillow.

"You're—leaving." It wasn't her words alone that silenced me; it was the cry of a child forsaken.

Helen, too, had changed. She had lost all of her glib certainty.

Turning back to Elva, we wondered how to say good-by. We wanted to give her the faith she needed. Her daughter clung to her hand. I touched Elva's forehead. "You have your daughter. She needs you."

John leaned over the bed. "Would you like us to send word to your husband before we go? He might still catch a boat." His voice was low and compassionate.

I nodded; the hope in her face spoke volumes. "If you'll just say the word, John will——"

Turmoil shook her. Finally she nodded, her voice so weak we had to bend close. "Tell him, please. Helen knows his address."

We did what we could for Elva and then rushed to board the boat.

The air was crisp as we began our trip down the Tanana River. "Do you think it's going to snow? We've hardly left the States." I pulled my coat closer.

"By the time we reach Pilot, the ground may be white."

"Now that we're getting near, I can't help wondering how it will seem to be back."

"I've been wondering the same—even while we were in the States."

"Some of the families will be coming back from the fishing banks."

"With any luck at all, the drying racks and the smokehouses will be full."

We heard a soft thud. "Boat's aground."

John joined the men to push the boat back into the channel. Using long poles, the men pushed and shoved away from the sand banks which shifted each year.

Snow fell, hiding the breadth of the river, as we continued downstream. The sky dimmed and the air was still. As I watched the falling snow and thought of the coming winter, I began to look forward to our arrival at Pilot Station.

John came to stand beside me. Something told me he too felt this new fascination. He looked at me with some bewilderment.

"I know you'll think I've gone crazy," he said, "but I'm anxious to see the dogs, the house and the village." We stood watching the river. "Remember how we zoomed down the bank? And trapped ptarmigan? And set the fishtraps?" He grinned in anticipation. "Never thought I'd be glad to see all that again!"

As the boat passed the old towns of Ruby, Galena and Nulato, huge fish wheels sloshed up and over, lifting the catch from the water; bobbing corks traced the water's surface above rippling nets. Everywhere we saw boats and kayaks pulled high on the beaches, fish-drying racks, "summer" tents of reindeer skins. Helen, the newcomer, was enthralled by the wilderness.

"Marshall is the next stop," John explained. "After that— home!"

Helen said, "Forty more miles, then you'll be gone, and I'll be on my own, just as I wanted to be!" She was both excited and nervous at the prospect. And still troubled by thoughts of Elva.

"Helen . . ." I touched her arm. "It won't be so bad." I didn't want to alarm her and I didn't want her to expect any more than she would find. It wouldn't be so bad, but it would not be an easy or a placid life.

She faltered. "I know. I know that now! But I never understood before." She bit her lip, then, "It's—I suppose I shouldn't have planned to come alone."

I reached for her hand. "Now that you know, you'll have something to plan for during the months ahead. This time next year you'll be getting married and coming straight back."

As the boat passed familiar landmarks, we fell silent, for Helen couldn't know how all these reminded us of the thrill of our first sled ride. "Home's just around the next bend!"

When we came in sight of Pilot Station, John called my attention to skin-covered tents pitched close to our house. "Who would be camping there this time of year?"

Ashore we found Burt waiting. John said, "Why in heaven's name are these tents here?"

Burt wouldn't tell us at once, but at last he said, "The bodies in the village, they stink—so we come here."

In dismay John said, "You mean the dead weren't buried this summer?"

"The bodies fall. The sun get hot. Everybody go away to fish."

"But you can't just leave them to rot!"

Burt, puzzled, shaking his head, went back to the tent.

Helen, silent, trailed me into the darkened house and stared at the heater, the daybed, the old chair, the desk. We passed into the kitchen and through Helen's eyes I saw the stove, the paint-chipped table, the water buckets and the tiny sink that spilled water through a trough to the ground outside. Propelled by Helen's adamant silence, I led her upstairs. She could not see these drab and drafty rooms as the place where Mae had been born. She saw the scratched bedstead, the dark-stained dresser and the closet with the stovepipe stabbing through. She followed me to the attic where food was stored, and then down the stairs, to the woodshed beyond, and the howling dogs tethered at their stakes.

She opened her mouth, and said nothing. I was impelled to protect what she saw. "It isn't as dreary as it looks," I told her. "It's what you make of it, really. Some of it may seem primitive, but it all makes sense up here. We can't have running water because of pipes freezing. And there's no well for the water to come from anyway, because just imagine trying to get water from a well when the whole Yukon freezes!"

She said, baffled, "But how do you make out?"

I couldn't answer her but I knew there were compensations. Like the saving of a life with an extra can of soup; like the warming of a tiny child in a hut bereft of heat; like the sight of peaceful sleep on a once-anguished face. But she wouldn't understand these things—not yet.

She clung to my hand as the boat whistled. "You can't ever know what these days with you have meant." She hesitated in a flood of useless words. And then she was gone, waving in fare-well, leaving me anxious for her first few months of loneliness.

Just then a boy came running with a note. "From Helen," I told John. "She must have sent it just as the boat pulled away."

"I've only a second," I read aloud, "but I want you to know that I'll never forget the lessons you've taught me. Helen."

Far out in the current the boat was a bobbing speck.

We entered the darkening house. Not even the tick of the long-stopped clock, the crackle of a long-cold stove or the sing-ing of a long-empty teakettle disturbed the calm. "If we had a fire, I'd make some coffee," I said at last, feeling the need to start building the semblance of home.

John rose as if glad for an excuse. Mae, waking, stared about. Solemnly she moved to the railing, sucking her thumb and twist-ing a knot of hair.

The night settled; a chill crept through the house. The room looked more desolate than ever and all that I'd tried to tell Helen seemed so many empty words. Tucking Mae into the wooden box bed, I bent over and kissed the little cheek, and at once the joy of having her reminded me of all we had. I went to John and put my arm through his. He looked down at me, clasping my hands in his. We turned toward the dark-blanketed bed and opened it.

"We always worry about the wrong things. They sometimes seem more important than the real ones." I sat down and began to get ready for bed. "Even now, so many months ahead, I keep wondering if we will really go back home in the spring or will we keep putting it off?"

I pulled the covers over us. "I think I worry mostly because of Mae."

John patted my arm. "Let's not get upset now—spring's a long way away."

Even as we drifted to sleep, I wondered what would come to us before the time of going home.

Chapter 18

THE NEXT DAY John rounded up the village men to help him dispose of what remained of the dead. Into shallow graves under a thin cover of earth and stone . . . After that, the Eskimo families moved back to their huts.

During our absence all supplies had been left on the beach. Now John carried them to the house where he and I sorted and stored barter goods, medical, school and personal supplies. One huge carton went to the attic; it contained old clothes sent by friends and relatives, to be wrapped as gifts for the villagers at Christmas.

"I wonder if we'll ever catch up," John said one morning. "It's time we butchered reindeer for winter meat."

"But with all the fish in the smokehouse, no one can be going hungry."

"They think they have eaten fish long enough."

I closed the cupboard door. "I suppose that means you'll be going."

"Time I went, Dolly."

I took Mae's new clothes upstairs to the dresser. When I came down John was waiting at the landing. "You must be dead tired," he said. "I'm sore enough from all this climbing and lugging."

These past two years had been a time of great responsibility, yet they had been a challenge too. Each crisis had brought us new problems, each had given us satisfaction and increased our self-reliance. We had renewed our reverence for humanity.

Outside, the dogs yapped for their evening meal. John went to feed them. While he was gone I thought of a man's two great desires—to have someone to care for and protect, and to have the freedom to test himself against the world.

When John came back he made me stop work. We'd done enough for one day. In two days, with luck, the butchering would be finished.

"You be careful while I'm gone," he reminded me, straightening from the packing. "Lock the doors."

And then, before morning broke over the hills, the boat chugged across the river. Mae and I, watching from the window, saw John appear at the wheel of the launch. While we stood waving, the boat dwindled, the blue smoke marking its going. The roar gentled in the distance.

Directly I turned to the chores of the day. For the next few hours I rubbed, soaked and scrubbed linens and woolens, feeling the sting of laundry soap on newly blistered knuckles. At my feet Mae played with an ivory doll. It had neither arms nor legs. Strands of fur made the hair; over its yellowing, scarred body was a miniature parka, fur-edged hood fitting close to the face, empty sleeves serving as arms.

Mae napped while I hung out the boiled clothes. Kobuk, looking up, nestled his head once more in his great gray paws. Midgie, the female, perked up her ears, then lay back contentedly on the sun-warmed earth.

At seven I finished supper. In the attic, boxes and cartons waited to be emptied. After locking doors and pushing more wood into the stove, I mounted the stairs with the coal oil lamp and came down again to carry Mae to bed. When I kissed her good night she clung to me. "Mae will sleep with me tonight," I reassured her. I put her into the big bed and pinned her safe. When Mae was asleep I tiptoed to the attic. The carton of clothes was my first job; between now and Christmas the clothing must be sorted and something laid aside for each member of the village.

Hours passed. At one in the morning, I climbed into bed, grateful for the job that had kept me so busy I'd had no time to worry.

The next afternoon the sun was hidden by a squall. The horizon darkened. I hurried to the yard to throw the dogs their supper. In my haste I forgot John's warning about locking all the doors. When I got back I found Joe, the half-breed, waiting inside the house. My knees knocked alarmingly; cold sweat dampened my hands. For a second I coudn't conceal my fear of him.

With knees still quaking I tried to speak in a normal tone. "You came for medicine, Joe?" I asked, moving slowly toward the medicine chest and away from him. "Is it headache or stomach-ache? Or maybe you cut yourself?" I wondered why he hadn't gone to the reindeer herd with the others.

How much I imagined, I don't know, but he looked crafty and cunning and up to no good. Why, oh why, hadn't I locked the door? "Aspirin? If you've got headache—" I continued to say anything that came into my head, rummaging in the cupboards—"maybe some liniment?"

I couldn't go on. I sensed he was closer.

Mae suddenly whimpered. I picked her up and held her in my arms. He touched her hair, met her staring eyes. "You— you have a little girl, too, Joe. Very pretty little girl. She looks like you, Joe."

I raised my voice, spoke more simply to be sure I had his attention. I mustn't stop. I had to distract him. He loved his child; the Eskimos cherished their children.

With that thought spinning in my head, I tried to get him to take Mae in his arms. "You see," I babbled, "she's like your little girl." My voice wavered.

And then, to keep Mae from being frightened, I said, "Daddy come, Daddy come."

Joe straightened, listening anxiously. Straightway he held out his hand. "Headache medicine!"

He left at once. I leaned briefly against the wall, then, at Mae's restrained whimper, I cuddled her in the old rocker, forcing myself to hum through tightened throat.

For an hour I rocked her, too tense to light the lamp or to move closer to the stove, forgetting in my panic to lock the door.

At last I got up, no longer able to delay Mae's bedtime. I heard a far-off rumble. With heart pounding, I waited, not daring to believe what that sound must mean. Even as it came nearer, the thought that my ears might be playing tricks kept me from racing into the darkness. I heard the dogs barking. I ran to the door and threw it wide, letting the newly lit lamp shine out to the men returning in the launch.

Yellow lights flared in the village; dogs howled and voices bellowed from the river in answer. Abruptly John was there, and I leaned against him in utter abandonment, all courage ebbing in my tears of relief. Hastily I dabbed at my eyes. He studied my face and seemed to guess what I'd been through.

The joy of having him with me was so great I immediately forgot the danger. But John said, "Tomorrow we're going out by the shed and you're going to learn to shoot the rifle. We won't quit practicing until everybody in the village knows you can."

He carried Mae upstairs. "Joe isn't one of our own; he comes and goes."

I looked at the gun in the rack behind the door. How could I ever learn to defend myself that way? I didn't want to live in fear when John was gone, but I didn't want to live in fear of doing injury to anyone.

There was more snow each day. A fawnskin parka and mittens were to be made for our baby by Oolinga, who tanned, scraped, chewed and worked the skin so that it would be soft and pliant.

Pancake ice appeared in the river. This new season meant that the men and women of the village must hurry to finish summer's chores, the mending of kayaks, nets, harnesses and sleds.

School began for the children—and for us. I could not bear to look at the two empty seats. Last year David's tiny, bony wrists had seemed too frail to support his hands. His face had grown so pitifully thin, I'd wanted to rest his tiredness against my heart. And Bobby—he'd fought so valiantly, as if his weakness spurred his dying body. Now both were dead.

And then there was Carmie, who still lingered. She was lying on a bed of reindeer skin in the lower village.

I was sick of this needless dying. Somehow we must do more to teach sanitation, repeating it, emphasizing it, dramatizing it, to these children. Especially to the girls, so that, when they had children, they could help. But it wasn't a change which could be made in a single generation.

When Mae's new parka was ready, I took her across the footbridge to the village. When they saw Mae in her winter dress, the grandmothers grinned toothlessly. Mae was the first white child born within their village; mothers, their own babies strapped on their backs, squatted eagerly beside Mae to touch her cheeks, to show their own children this child whose hair was blond and skin pale.

Our friend Jim showed us his catch of blackfish. I praised his skill. I led Mae down the trail, past an abandoned log house built by some miner, past the round smokehouse where the golden salmon hung, past a leaning hut with a single high window dimmed by smoke, where a widower lived with his two children, indifferent to the stench and filth.

John came down the trail, calling to Mae, and swung the crowing child to his shoulder. "Just a few more cold nights like this, and there'll be no more pancake ice," John said to me.

He was right; presently the river slept. At its peace we stood awed. In every direction this prostrate giant now lay humbled. Hills, trees, bushes, streams, lay at peace. It was a world wrapped in eternity. Pondering this silence, so deep it had no echoing, so deep it had no ending, we felt the loneliness that comes when no living thing lifts its voice, when no cry or blast or trumpet comes from the hillside to stir the heart.

With Thanksgiving so close, we kept busy. A fat crane John had shot hung frozen on the porch. John took over the schoolroom one day while I searched the cookbooks for a miracle that would change our daily fare into something less monotonous.

But even though I could find no such recipe, there were some variations to make us forget a diet of fish and reindeer meat. In the evening we visited cozily at the square kitchen table, not caring that a blizzard had begun. Inside, we laughed in the glow of the flickering lamp, munching cookies and nuts brought from home and drinking the coffee we'd grown to depend upon.

Thanksgiving morning was clear; a brilliant sun shone. Together we stuffed the crane. Mae was old enough to sense our holiday excitement. John couldn't keep her out of the fragrant kitchen.

"Not a guest to help us eat our crane!" John hoisted the brown bird from the oven. I began to make gravy. We were silent, both thinking of home.

John carried the platter to the table and began to carve the breast, laying the slabs side by side. Mae clamored to see. I picked her up gently, kissing her, then put her into the high chair John had hammered together. Her pink, ruffled dress and long white stockings, her clumsy mukluks . . .

After John had asked the blessing, he kissed us both. "I'm grateful," he said, "for all God has granted us."

We took our first taste of the crane, watching each other for a sign of disappointment or satisfaction.

"It's tender," John said, "but not quite turkey."

"At least it isn't reindeer!" I gave Mae a taste, but she spit it out. "She ate very little cereal this morning," I said rather anxiously. "Do you think she's got a temperature?"

John touched her forehead. "Her skin is hot." We were so accustomed to the swarthy complexions of the Eskimo children that Mae always looked too pale or too flushed.

While the pie was being served, John's glance strayed repeatedly to Mae's thin fingers pulling her hair gently as she grew sleepy. He lifted her to his lap, cuddling and petting her, talking softly until she went to sleep.

"She needs fresh air. But we have to keep the windows tight-shut." If we bundled her well, we could take her into the village, but then we would not dare leave her alone in the sled; and it would be dangerous to take her into any of the huts. I left her alone when school was in session, crossing the hall now and then to be sure she was safe. But even so I might be carrying infection from the children in the class.

"Even my coming in to see her at noon and during recess might not be good, but I can't leave her to herself so long."

John said, "You know, even we don't get enough fresh air. We should get outside to clear our lungs. We aren't immune to germs."

"Every time you go into the village to look after the sick, I worry that you might catch something."

John poured more coffee, and we went into the other room where Mae slept.

"Don't wake her," John said. "With God's help we'll raise her to be a fine girl, and someday we'll realize how useless worry is."

"Every day, when the weather is good, we'll try to get out for a walk."

We heard steps and a knock. John answered and came back hurriedly, pulling on his parka. "It's Big Mike. Sounds like blood poisoning. I'll be back as soon as I can."

I watched the dog team racing down the hill to the trail, heard John's voice calling to the dogs. What a contrast to our months of vacation such a short time ago! Here life was precious because it was so precarious. Emergencies meant an immediate response or the danger of death.

I went to the kitchen to wash the dishes and to await John's return. Would he be able to save the old man? Perhaps a doctor could, but could John with so little to work with? Old Mike probably had consulted the medicine man, had perhaps waited too long before coming to John for help, and might, even after John tended him, take the medicine man's advice and chew willow bark, the only remedy they seemed to trust.

Darkness had come before John returned, even though the afternoon had hardly begun. "What was it?" I asked as he pulled off his parka.

"Blood poisoning. Cut his thumb when he was taking fish out of the trap."

"Was the medicine man there?" I poured hot water in a pan so John could scrub himself.

"He had been. Mike's hand is badly swollen. I soaked it in bichloride of mercury, but it may not help." Together we sat before the heater, our Thanksgiving Day so suddenly ended. "Tomorrow I'll go over again."

For two days John tended Old Mike's hand, using hot packs, Epsom salts and mercury, staying close to guard against the pain—and to see that the medicine man had no chance to interfere with the treatment.

In other huts John gave remedies for swollen joints, colds and constipation.

The little Eskimo girl, so ill, continued to worry me. "I suppose there's no change in Carmie?" I asked.

John sat down at the kitchen table. "No. She's no thinner, but her cough is bad."

"Can she sit up?" I saw the hollow eyes, the gaunt ribs.

"Sometimes she tries to when I go in, but it's too much effort. She begins to cough."

"I'll send more soup. Maybe next time she'll eat a bit."

That evening we began sorting the old clothes in the attic, the Christmas gifts we planned. "Let's wrap some this evening. Before long we'll have to begin getting ready for the Christmas feast."

So, with Mae, we climbed to the attic. By lamplight we worked, hoping that the little we could do would, somehow, make up for all that was not in our power to accomplish.

Chapter 19

THE DAYS RACED toward Christmas. We worked long hours in the cold attic and in the schoolroom. But finally, on the day of the Christmas program, great chains of colored paper stretched across the windows, ropes of popcorn hung on the tree, and on the floor were piled our gifts, the bundles of clothing. As night came, the Northern Lights filled the sky with gay, rampant color, stretching sharp fingers above the horizon, displaying their colors brilliantly against the sky's boundless canvas. Soon dog teams arrived. Almost instantly the schoolroom filled, the clamor and excitement repaying us tenfold for the weeks of preparation.

As the program began, we noticed one friend missing—a young girl who seldom left the family hut, not even in the spring when the other children went fishing.

We forgot her for a time as we enjoyed the squeals of delight. New clothes were tried on and each new bundle unwrapped and displayed. Then at last, as the evening came to an end, the mothers pulled hoods high, the men buttoned their jackets, the boys and girls stood awkward and proud in their new shoes. Brown hands clasped ours. When the last dog team raced away, we sank down exhausted, pleased at how well the party had gone. Not a package remained. Even the absent girl would have her bundle. The floor of the schoolroom was swamped in wrapping paper. John rose wearily. Tired as we were, we would have to clean up the mess before tomorrow's feast. Hours later we fell exhausted into bed.

By noon the next day the village had arrived for the feast. By three o'clock every bit of food was gone. Leftovers had been wrapped and taken home to the sick; tubs of stew had vanished; there wasn't a crust of bread left behind. It was like feeding a hundred voracious sparrows.

After such an ordeal our own Christmas dinner seemed an anticlimax, a letdown for its usualness. "Some day," I told John, "we'll have a real family Christmas in our own home."

John bent over the washpan, soaping himself thoroughly. "We make our own Christmas, wherever we are. We've had two high old days, and that's more than we've a right to boast."

We sat at the table. I put the biscuits before him. "What would it be like," I said, "if we didn't really get on with each other?"

"That's one thing we'll never worry about! Tonight we'll celebrate as if we were in the States. There are a few packages, and this is the first Christmas when Mae is old enough to know it's a special time."

After dinner, with the needle on the school's old phonograph scratching out the dear, beloved carols, we sat near the roaring stove, singing the familiar songs because singing was a part of our way of remembering the season. When we brought out the packages, Mae was silent with delight. She had to touch everything. Her own gifts from home, a bracelet and a ring, she hardly noticed in the confusion of bright paper and boxes.

"I see now why our baggage was bulging," John said. We each had a new watch, guaranteed to run no matter what the weather.

The day was about to end—our last Christmas in Alaska. Tomorrow the problem of the sick would be no nearer solution. They lay in rooms filled with the chores of the living, finding neither rest nor quiet. Nor did the presence of the sick help the others in their struggle to live, for it was no easy task to hold to routine, preparing meals on a simple stove in a room given over to the spirit of pain, the sound of suffering, the silence of unconsciousness or depression.

"We'll go with you," I told John one day as he was making ready for a visit in the village. "We'll stay in the sled while you make your calls."

He checked the thermometer hanging just outside the door. "It's forty below. You'll have to wrap up well."

We waited in the sled while he entered hut after hut. At his knock doors opened, dark faces appeared. On down the row of huts he went. He stayed in Carmie's house a long time.

Carmie, that gentle girl, was dead—her eyes shut, her hands still, her thin breast motionless, the worn parka covering her. My pity for such suffering I could not express except by hugging our child closer.

When John finally emerged from the hut, his face was lined with sorrow. As he unleashed the dogs, I said, "She's gone."

He nodded. "The medicine man was there. When they moved her, I saw the last box of pills I'd taken her under the reindeer skin. They might have spared her this last pain."

The dogs jumped to his command. Mae pointed and laughed at the rushing team, imitating John's commands of *mush*, *gee*, and *haw* from the folds of her parka.

As John unhitched the dogs, I said, "We'll make some hot cocoa."

As we sat close to the stove, the village dogs filled the silence with their voices. I rushed to the window. "It's a large team!" I said.

"Must be the mailman. No one else would be traveling in this weather." John held Mae close to the window and pointed out the dog sled coming across the frozen river. He wiped the steam from the cloudy window pane. "The mail order catalogue will have a rest for a few days. Guess we've thumbed through and priced every page till we know it all by heart!"

We used the catalogue to teach the Eskimo children the names and look of objects they had never seen. One girl, Lucy, fell in love with a picture of an electric stove—it was to her the most beautiful stove she could possibly imagine. And perhaps catalogues of this sort will do more than all the teachers in encouraging young Eskimos to better their condition.

"Perhaps someday—who knows—more of these people will do as Johnny Sun did—go to the Indian School in Oregon for a few years."

But when he returned, within a few weeks, he discarded the white corduroys and the neat shirts, the shined shoes. He did not feel a part of the village until he wore parka and boots again.

The dog team climbed the bank. As soon as the mail was inside and sorted, we fell to with gusto, opening the letters from the Indian Bureau first. Family letters were our dessert.

"More records from the main office. A note from the Smithsonian Institution. They'd like us to collect artifacts that we think might be of value."

"And a notice about payments on the beach property." This was land my parents had urged us to buy, a wooded spot across from Seattle, deep in the country, where one day we would relax, free of mosquitoes, free of this land of ice and snow.

John held out another letter. "From Ethel and Stan Gray. They're here in Alaska!"

The young couple who had come to see us at the farm last summer, planning their honeymoon, applying for jobs at a wilderness school, following our example, heedless of our warning that the life would be hard.

John tore open the letter. "From Ethel. It was written several weeks ago. She's probably lonesome for news of people she knows."

I took the folded letter from him, recalling Ethel's vivacity, her fragile figure, her devotion to Stan. I dropped my eyes to the letter. "Dear friends—This is to tell you about Stan . . ."

John saw the change in me. He reached for the letter and read it through. I could hear their ardent voices planning. What had she said about their being all alone? Whatever their hopes, none mattered now.

"Perhaps you've already heard that Stan is dead." And then, painfully, scrupulously, Ethel described his death. With a new team he had gone out on the trail. The sled had broken through a weak place in the ice. Ethel waited. When evening came, she sent others out to look for him. Within moments they found him, rigid, huddled against the sled he'd pulled from the water. Knowing how quickly one could freeze, he'd tried to dry and warm himself, safety and a blazing stove lying just beyond the next bend. Burned matches were scattered here and there. One wet mukluk was clasped in his hand; a frozen sock was half on one foot. Dry clothes from his pack lay on the ice. In those few moments he had frozen.

John came to the end of the letter. "His body is in the shed, waiting for the first boat. I pray to God."

But before the first boat reached the settlement, Stan's body would have to be buried in the land where he died.

I remembered last spring, when John had risked his life in a kayak, our trips across the flatlands in a storm. How often we had endangered ourselves needlessly, how lucky we were to have escaped!

Poor Ethel. Our sympathy could not help.

Our letters from home had to wait. We could not absorb them with the tragedy of Stan's death so fresh in our minds. And each letter now would ask the question: Are you coming home for good? Neither of us dared mention leaving, for there were months before we could go and we had no heart to plan so far ahead, perhaps to be disappointed. But we knew that for many days we would see Stan's frozen body and the distraught girl by his side. Ethel's helplessness became our own.

As the weeks passed, we were glad to have so many duties and chores. The village meat supply decreased with the longer days. "I'd like to make an icehouse," John said, "and have it finished for the next butchering. In fact, two more trips to the reindeer camp should last us to the break-up."

I'd been dreading the time John would leave on such a trip.

"You might have someone stay with you while I'm gone. In fact, I've been thinking you should have someone to help."

I shook my head. "No. There's no one."

"The Suns have the least sickness. Or someone from Grace's family."

"I don't know." Yet he was right in saying I needed help. Perhaps if Clara Sun kept well . . .

"Lock your doors early," John said, after packing for the deer camp. He kissed Mae good-by. "And, Dolly, feed the young dogs early, and if anyone comes to the door, shout a warning and then shoot if the warning isn't enough."

He kissed me, then hugged us both.

"Be careful, darling," I called. John waved to us; Kobuk shook the harness. "And you, Kobuk—come home safe!"

I shut the door to keep myself from watching the sled go. "Two days to be alone," I told Mae, "and two nights. By Monday he should be home!" She followed me to the kitchen and trailed me as I cleaned house.

When evening came, I stoked the fire with wood I'd brought in early, double-checked all doors and windows and went upstairs where I felt less likely to be spied upon.

The night glittered with cold. The moon cast queer shadows against the folded earth. I stood at the window, hearing sounds which would have gone unheeded if John had been at home. Below the window snow lay high against the house. Because, though dark, it was too early to sleep, I thumbed through the mail order catalogue, realizing suddenly that, if we were going back to the States, now was the time to order clothing. Entranced, I chose Mae's coat and bonnet, John's shirts and socks; I needed a coat, hat, shoes. But while the coats were confusing enough to select from a picture, the hats were even more baffling. How did one choose between them? Resigned, I jotted down the number of a cherry-brimmed hat, a princess-style coat, medium-heeled shoes. Doubts soared again: the hat's brim could be a shocking, floppy thing, always in my eyes; my shoe size might have increased after the unhampered ease of mukluks. Midnight! I closed the catalogue and blew out the lamp, relieved that the job was done.

Much, much later I woke, listening, frozen still by a sound I did not recognize. Trembling, I brought Mae closer, waiting for the sound to come again.

Then I heard it more clearly. The sound brought me instantly to a sitting position. I crept down to the door and reached for the gun. In the moon's shadowy light, I put the gun near by on the table and sat down, shivering with a chill that would not stop.

It was nearly two. Wishing desperately that this night of darkness were over, I sat hugging my arms and trying to still my chattering teeth. But no amount of hoping could make daylight come any faster.

Sitting in the chair, my eyes sore with wakefulness, I heard the creak come again, hesitantly, as if my own heart could be heard outside. And then the steps were more distinct, and suddenly out of the blackness of my fear I knew they came from the path directly below the window.

I listened until I could barely breathe. Had I bolted all the windows? Had the slab of timber that held shut the door of the shed been tested? And one windowpane was cracked. Could someone outside guess how easily it would shatter?

Swiftly, unable to stop myself, I raced to the window. And I remembered there was a ladder somewhere. A ladder would reach to the cracked window.

Silence again. Chills crept up my back; my knees were shaking so violently that I reached down to steady them. The gun is here. The doors are locked and bolted. But the chills grew more intense.

A dog cried in the night and another answered. I crept back to the chair; the moon's light threw shadows. Paralyzing fright gripped me. Briefly I hid my face in my hands.

I looked at the clock. Why was this night so long, the minutes so slow in their passing? I pressed unsteady fingers to my temples, trying not to listen yet hearing the sound of slow footsteps. Mae moved and cried out. I went up to her and found her hand and spoke in a voice that did not rise above a whisper.

Touching Mae gave me courage. If I had to fire, it would be in defense of my child. I stood beside the table where the gun lay. Over and over, John's warning words came to me: "Shoot to scare."

Now the thought did not frighten me. The need to protect Mae was uppermost, obliterating my terror of the gun. I found a sweater and put it under my robe. I tried to cuddle into it against the bitter chill of the room.

Three-thirty! I could hear no sound of a ladder against the side of the house. Surely in the stillness I would hear splintering glass or pressure against the door.

Gradually the sky grew pale. Chattering with cold, I put the gun back in the rack and crept into bed. The night was over. I felt wretchedly tired; my temples throbbed, my arms and legs felt drained of all energy. I closed my eyes, glad for the light of morning.

Chapter 20

I BREAKFASTED LATE, then turned to my work. Mae's slips and dresses must be lengthened. And in this way I put from my mind all thought of the night before. Before dusk John would be home. In a few weeks, a few months, we would be leaving this place for good. With the thought of summer came visions of warmth returning Outside—new-furrowed fields, fresh green of wild plum trees, the white-vested swallow.

I roused myself. Up here, too, spring must come. Already the mercury hovered at zero. Soon water would rise along the banks, allowing the foraging muskrat to find his prey. School would come to an end, and the families would leave for the fishing camps.

A knock interrupted me. Johnny Sun waited. "My father wonder if his furs can be sent pretty soon now."

"As soon as the men return, Johnny. Has he many?"

"Very many. Fox, mink, muskrat."

I remembered Johnny Sun's sister Clara and the suggestion that one of the family might help us. I asked about her.

"Last week she has cough, but now much better."

The day passed before I could decide to call on Clara, and by evening I knew John would not be home that night. I fed the dogs hurriedly, then locked the shed more securely than ever before. The other doors I had kept locked during the day. After dinner I went quickly upstairs. Last night's clear moon was gone. The night was black. The coming storm threatened to be a raging blizzard by morning. Holding Mae close, I breathed a prayer that John would be safe at the reindeer camp on this harsh night.

I answered letters until twelve. Snow was settling over the trail, covering the landmarks, smothering the high banks that the teams used as guides. John wouldn't be coming home until tomorrow. But if he feared for our safety? I brought the covers high. Would John take the chance? I shivered.

I couldn't keep from my mind the thought of Stan, frozen. Never thinking it could happen to him. Would John remember Ethel's letter? I tossed wretchedly. No. In the depth of his concern, he'd forget the dangers on the blizzard-swept trail. Surely John would not leave the protection of the reindeer camp. He'd realize Kobuk's inexperience; he must know, in spite of his worry, that the cutting lash of the wind, the obliterated trail, the country become unchartered, unfamiliar, would break the strongest man.

I tucked Mae closer, feeling her warmth. I closed my eyes. Sleep would put an end to the ways a mind can torment itself.

But sleep did not come and this was not morning. Doubt possessed me. Was he out on the trail or safe in camp? Perhaps he left camp before the storm began? I pushed the blankets away. I struggled to control my thinking in the face of anguish.

As the hours passed and fatigue numbed thought, the dark room became the trail. I saw a figure trudging, head bent against the blizzard, his face lifted now and then as he sought a land-mark. I tried to call to him, but I made no sound. I heard him call to the dogs, but they refused to obey. The dogs floundered and crouched stubbornly as the man staggered and almost fell. I hid my face in agony at his faltering steps. The whip swung feebly; the lead dog laid back his ears in defiance. Weaker now, the man fell, got up, fell again. The wind drove at him in wrath. I hid my eyes as he fell.

I woke with a scream.

I lay back, too spent to care. Apprehension gave place to apathy. I pulled Mae closer.

The need for movement, for light in the darkened room, was urgent. The flickering lamp brought no relief. When I woke from that strange night, it was as if a nightmare had wrung my heart dry. I tried to throw off the depression but the night's battle had been too vivid to disregard.

Downstairs, while the stove roared, I talked to Mae, telling her how soon she would see her father. At eight-thirty I rang the school bell. The sound of it, reverberating, was the release I needed. I reached for the rope once more. At its final hush-ing I waited for the children to appear. I felt the blast of cold air and re-entered the hall, momentarily oblivious to every-thing but the dying sound of the bell.

I stood breathless, hearing the sound of dogs but not yielding to its familiarity, for suddenly the night's fears returned. I heard the dogs yapping but it was like a mockery. And then abruptly I went to the window.

I saw the team hobbling on the river ice. The figure guiding the sled wavered and struggled to hang on. I saw the snow-stiffened parka, the frost on his eyebrows, the ravaged face. He raised one arm in greeting as the team pulled into the yard. I saw him stagger. But John was safe. And I went to him to help him into the house.

Inside, Mae began to cry. Before I could stop her she crawled into his snowy lap. I pulled off his mukluks and tugged at his parka, begging him to help me. I brought hot coffee. After a while he grinned. His weary eyes were nearly shut. In silence we sat close to one another.

At noon John woke when I came from the schoolroom, and again at three. I smoothed the hair from his forehead.

"Last night I dreamed you were out in that blizzard. Like Stan. I thought I heard you calling to me, and I tried to run to you."

He took my hand. "And all the while I was glad you didn't know!" His fingers tightened. "When I left camp, there wasn't a storm. After a while, when the clouds came up, I thought of turning back, but by then it was too late. Last night, when nothing was left to point the way, Kobuk—" he glanced up— "Kobuk kept veering to the right, but I was sure the tall, crooked tree I was looking for was to our left. I was afraid he was trying to take me in the wrong direction. And the closest village would have been too far away. It was a battle between the two of us. He'd always obeyed me before, but in a blizzard he was defiant. I even used the whip, but he wouldn't let me turn us to the left."

"And you couldn't decide to trust his judgment?"

"I even pulled him around by the collar, but as soon as I waded back to the sled, he veered again. Once or twice I fell. When I did, Kobuk licked my face. That should have told me he wasn't simply refusing to obey but was doing his best to guide us home. After that, I guess, my mind got hazy. I couldn't fight Kobuk any more. I crouched in the sled thinking of you and Mae! I was very tired and wanted to rest. The thought frightened me."

John reached for Mae, bringing her close to his whiskery face. He hid his face in the angle of her neck.

"If it hadn't been for Kobuk," John said. "He was willing to be whipped—even willing to fight me for our lives, thank God for that! And then something sent you out to ring the school bell. I heard it. I knew Kobuk was bringing us home."

I sat back, tears slowly gathering in my eyes. I could think of only one thing to say. "God bless him, God bless him!"

I'd always been somewhat afraid of the dogs. They seemed wild, vicious, closer to wolves than the pets I had known at home. Now I went to Kobuk, calling his name, venturing to touch him. And he rewarded me by wagging his tail.

For the rest of the day I was never far from John. Seeking his thoughts once, I turned toward him, but his look silenced me; his thoughts were his own and the struggle deep.

He spoke finally, without looking at me. "It's time we sent for money in case we decide to go back to the States."

He looked at the river. "Spring is just around the corner. There probably won't be another big storm. I want to finish the icehouse so it'll be ready for fish and meat. Whoever takes our place up here will be glad of it."

"And the team. Shouldn't you try to sell the dogs?" The moment I spoke I knew it was the wrong time. Having so lately been grateful to Kobuk for John's life, I should not have shown how anxious I was to leave Alaska.

John paused; I realized what a loss this would be to him.

I reached for his hand. "Someone will be glad to have them, if we do go."

He looked up quickly. "You mean—we might not go?"

"We haven't decided definitely." I could say it now, but an hour ago if John had urged we stay—— A week, a month ago, there had been no doubt in my mind that we ought to get away. But now, with Kobuk, and John's apparent sense of regret . . .

I looked from the window to our tightly clasped hands. I couldn't raise my eyes.

"If we go, all the records have to be filled out; the specimens for the Smithsonian Institution shipped; Sun's furs packed. And our own things," John said.

"I've made out an order for clothes we ought to buy."

He said, "You're really planning on it, aren't you, Dolly?" At my nod he went on. "I know. I don't blame you. And I know we should go." He looked at the bare walls. "Here, we're settled, with no real worries. Outside, I'll have to scrape up some job, find some way to live."

"In another year it would be even harder to get established." I remembered the faces of those we'd met in Alaska, all somewhat fearful of the world they'd left behind. Over the years they'd forgotten the freshness of soft rain on roses, the warmth of living with others.

I was unable to put these things into words, for I understood John's silent argument. In the States we must turn to a new sort of future, one which often seemed nothing but competition. Never quite attaining a goal, often uncertain of what our goal was, never quite fulfilling society's expectations, or our own, never quite at peace with our hearts and souls in a country so clamorous, so feverish, so impatient for change in the name of progress. Here, on the other hand, were people who needed us. Here, too, already lay an important part of our lives—a certain richness and serenity for all its simplicity and rawness. What mattered here were life and death, not promotion and opinion.

John rose with Mae in his arms. He saw no shackles in this primitive village. I saw how much our child would lack. He reached for my hand. "Come on, darling, it's time for bed."

I followed. Our future had not been settled; we needn't decide at once. But soon the river would open to the ocean. Then we must either leave, as I wished, or wait for another spring—or yet another.

Chapter 21

THE DAYS SEPARATING US from spring came more quickly than I could have imagined. The tasks seemed to multiply each day.

"It's a good time to have Clara," John said.

With Clara to help in the house, John and I turned our attention to the many reports we had to complete whether we left Pilot Station or not. We spent hours describing the progress of the school, the state of the village, the size of the reindeer herds, the prospect of plenty or starvation.

"The new fawns will have to be marked," John said. "Last year the ravens came too early, before there was food, and attacked the young. Terrible loss."

"Can't the villagers protect the newborn?"

John glanced up from his report. "Not once they've been set on. They don't last that long!" He snapped his fingers in emphasis.

I'd heard but not seen what had happened. The ravens blinded the young deer and waited for them to wander off from the herd. Those not killed by the ravens were attacked by wolf packs or a scavenger fox.

"A shame," John admitted, "but animals must prey on one another. We can't do much to prevent it. Better by far to worry over the sick in the village. There we can help." He went back to his papers.

I put Mae to bed while he finished. She clung to me, her face so pale she seemed always on the verge of fever or chill. When I returned to the kitchen, Clara straightened from the counter, her face stained with berry pie. I saw the empty pie plate.

"You like pie?" I asked inanely. It was not gluttony but ever-present hunger.

She looked at me blankly. Even the meat platter was empty. "You full now?" I remembered her shyness at mealtime, unwilling to accept second helpings.

She smiled at that, rubbing her stomach. "Yes. Plenty full," she confessed.

Hours later, after we'd got to bed, the muffled coughing began. Instantly tense, we wakened. Was it Mae? No, it was Clara. The cough was hollow, deep. The next morning, only one thought was uppermost; we must get Clara out of the house and see that she was cared for at home. After breakfast John told her she must go. She stared at him blankly, the circles under her eyes more pronounced. We gave her food and some spare clothing.

"You must have rest," John explained gently. "When you get well, maybe someday you come back." I brought her parka and helped her with it.

We watched her as she walked slowly across the bridge, hugging to her chest the things we had given her. I thought of the ravens following the blind fawn and saw death following Clara across the high bridge.

"She won't get well," I said. "She may live another twenty years, but she won't get well."

With antiseptic, John scrubbed the doorknobs and kitchen utensils. Whatever she had touched was boiled. And all the while, as the steam filled the kitchen, the futility of our protest against the diseases of poverty, illiteracy and superstition remained an ironic comment on our three years of effort.

So powerful in effect was Clara's illness that it swept all prior arguments aside. Before, when we considered the possibility of leaving, our success in helping some of the villagers softened and deterred us. Our services were of some value. But now this issue seemed irrelevant. We must leave this sick land before one of us—perhaps Mae—died of it. Clara's hopeless condition filled me with a dread I could not conquer, a sense of utter despair.

"John," I said, "let's take the first boat home."

I knew all the thoughts that must be running through his mind, but now they did not count. I remembered that day, three years before, when we boarded the government boat *Boxer*. We were coming to a land where people needed our help. We were anxious to put into practice our college training. We wanted to minister to those who struggle alone. And during our stay—birth, sickness, the hours when the light of life flickered and died—during all those weeks, months and years, caring for them in their weakness, sometimes despising them for their carelessness, reprimanding them as one does a naughty child, we grew to love them.

Blinded by this duty of love, we forgot what we owed each

other and our child; or at least we postponed self-concern, as if realizing that our own circumstances were of little or no importance in the face of those in greater need.

But now Clara as she crossed the deserted bridge made me see Mae as she might be a few years hence, crossing another bridge into a dark land we might have saved her from. In the prospect of this future I could be firm in saying we'd done all we were able to do for our village.

Together John and I watched Mae run about the room. It did not seem possible she was growing up so fast.

It was such a stark and simple room. The curtains hung limp, their rips no longer hidden in the skimpy folds; the walls so drab I shuddered; the scarred desk, the ugly chairs, the ugly heater. For two years I'd ignored how I hated to live like this.

John saw my growing discontent. "Say it, Dolly," he prompted. "I can tell what you're thinking. You'd give anything to leave tomorrow."

I shook my head, helpless in the thought that whatever I said could have been said at any time during the three years, and, because it had not been said at once, it was useless to say it now.

John said, impatiently, "Why the sudden decision? Nothing's really changed—the same sicknesses, the same chores! Why decide now?"

"I know, John, but, well—if we can't decide now, how will we ever decide?"

John stood at the stove, warming his hands. "I've been wondering the same, Dolly." He looked at me, helplessly. "I don't feel ready to make a decision that we'll always wonder about, never being sure we've chosen right. Just look what happened on the trail with Kobuk. It's the same sort of choice now, in a way."

I nodded. If a decision had to be made, passing impulse might help us to discover what we really wanted in the future. John, first laughingly, then more seriously, suggested we flip a coin. But for a time we would go on as we were, completing our chores in the village.

"Did you finish packing Sun's furs for shipment?" I asked. Furs had to be sorted, labeled and sacked.

"We'll finish today." John brightened; he grinned and went out to the shed. He came back with a big box, clumsily wrapped. "A belated happy birthday—many months overdue." He put the box on my lap.

"Open it, Dolly."

I found inside a beautiful fox fur, by far the best of those the Sun family were shipping for sale in the States. I held it to my cheek and stroked the fur.

"Sun said you could exchange it for another if you want to," John said.

"No," I said. "No. John, it's lovely." And I kissed him.

A week later it was time to close the school. We stood in the doorway as the children left. Each one tried to thank us as we said good-by. Next year which of these little ones would not return? During the summer one might die. And next winter? Another and another. They had come to us, and we had done what we could. Had we fulfilled our trust? Had we accomplished something, given them hope and courage and faith as well as kindness? Remembering the past months, we felt we had reason to be encouraged. And after that we closed the door.

Almost overnight the village emptied. The men were going to hunt muskrats. Some of the women remained, but we saw nothing of the paralyzed girl who had been too ill to come to our

Christmas party. We met Burt on the trail and asked him what had happened to the girl. Had she gone too?

Burt shrugged. The girl was there in the house. She was going to have a baby. All the women stayed away because they believed that her blood was bad and it would harm them to touch her.

"She's alone?" I said, indignantly.

He nodded. "You only look in window."

John would not let me go to her, fearing infection, but he took me home and hurried back.

As he grew accustomed to the shadows, he saw the girl huddling in a corner, covered with a reindeer skin. He spoke to her, but she did not answer. She seemed to be unconscious. He studied the pale face under the matted hair, heard the heavy breathing. Leaning over her, he watched her face for a sign she was in labor. The stench was overpowering. All about seemed to be the finality of death. The girl's hands lay clasped at her young, gaunt breast. Dried blood had caked on the reindeer coverlet. Overwhelmed at the pitiful sight, John did not at once attempt to feel her pulse. He was certain she was near death.

He bent over her again, uncovering her face, looking for some life in her dulled eyes. He straightened, then stepped to the door to fill his lungs with uncontaminated air.

Repeatedly he moved from the dense odor to the door, then stooped to re-enter the hovel. He leaned over her, fearful that she had died in the battle to give life. A foul odor made him retch and gasp. He stayed beside her through the night, bathing her forehead, keeping a fire lit.

At dawn he stretched, feeling the lameness of a tall man

forced to crouch for warmth. He bent over the wasted figure, touching the pale forehead.

He looked about; no food in the house, the water all but gone. He went outside, filling his lungs. Then he climbed aboard the sled.

At home he left the stinking parka outside. In the woodshed he bathed in hot water and antiseptic. Heavy-eyed, he sat for breakfast but he could not swallow and could barely tell me what he had been through.

"I've got to go back, Dolly. If you'll put some coffee in the thermos, and give me some soup to take, I'll try to wake her and get her to eat."

The medical book warned about exhaustion and lack of sleep. "Promise you'll come back and go to bed," I pleaded.

At noon he returned and napped briefly. "You must rest," I told him. "If labor hasn't started, you can't hurry it."

John was puzzled. "I don't understand it. She was supposed to be in labor."

"Maybe she isn't due yet."

He ate, then prepared to continue his vigil. "I admit I'm not doing any good, but maybe my being there gives her some kind of comfort."

He went back to the hut. Standing beside the bed, he studied her carefully. She was like a wizened child. John found it impossible to believe that she was pregnant. He sat beside her waiting, listening for a sigh, hearing only the rustle of the wind against the hut. He stayed through the night, not certain if she were alive.

Two o'clock . . . three . . . dawn crept inside the fetid room. Suddenly John knelt at her side. Abruptly he flung the deerskin from her, and the sight that met his eyes staggered him. The baby lay at the girl's thighs, the afterbirth still clinging to her withered body. She had borne this child without the help or the presence of anyone. Here she had lain because none of the village women would come near her during the ordeal.

John realized the birth must have occurred the day Burt told him of it; the women had known even as they watched through the window. Superstition had kept them away.

After a time, when the shock had lessened, he began to bathe the girl. He boiled water and came home for cloths, soap and antiseptic. He would not come in the house but asked me to pass him what he needed. He hardly spoke; the sunken eyes, lined face and grimy hands told more than words.

When the job was done, he came home but he felt he could not rid himself of the odor of death. He scrubbed himself vigorously but at dinner he left the table, too ill to eat. It was not until morning that we could talk of the gentle girl who had struggled alone.

The snow, under the warmer sun, sank lower. Swelling rivulets traced gullies into the growing river. Everywhere were signs of spring—the migrant goose, the swelling buds, warmer winds playing over the trail.

Honeycomb ice was a danger for the unwary. One misstep into that rotten ice and dogs, sled and driver would flounder and sink. Nevertheless, the hunt for ducks and geese did not slacken. In spite of my protests, John went hunting alone.

John was silent when he returned from the hunt—a silence I had learned to question. I looked at the array of ducks and geese—it wasn't disappointment at the game he'd brought back.

He kissed me then. As he did so I saw that his parka was soaked and clinging to him.

"John . . ." For a moment Ethel's anguished cry came through the silence.

John tried to calm me. "It was nothing. I shot some geese, and the dogs started after them, pulling the sled. I grabbed at the sled as it went by and tried to hold them back. Can't figure yet what got into them."

I was shaking uncontrollably. "And there was honeycomb ice."

He knelt beside the couch and looked at the sleeping baby, caressing her with his glance as he often did.

"I knew the bad ice was close," he said, "and so did Kobuk, but for half a second . . ." he paused, then went on, "When Kobuk remembered, he veered away. Just that slight turn saved us, I guess. The ice crumpled as the sled touched it, but the dogs scrambled to safe ground."

I brought dry slippers and socks. He was soaked to the knees and needed a complete change of clothing. "Now," I said, "we're going to flip that coin." And I handed him a coin.

He looked up, bewildered. "Now?"

I said, "Yes, now."

He took the coin, sent it spinning over our heads, caught it. He held his hand over the coin until I said, "Heads we leave, tails we stay."

We stared at the coin, unable to force sounds from our tense throats. It was heads.

John saw my look of relief, but he could not help provoking me. "We ought to make it two out of three." Before I could stop him, he flipped the coin high. My heart thudded.

John opened his hand, then closed it again before I could see the coin. "That's not fair," I said, and forced him to open his hand. The coin lay heads up.

How often, when you've wanted something so long and so desperately, some of the gladness goes out of it when you get your wish. It's lost somehow in the waiting or in the doubts that follow the first anticipation. So it was at that moment, when I knew we were free to go.

I went to John. "We don't have to," I said. "Nothing's been really decided."

"Even I won't go against two out of three," he said. "We'll be leaving as soon as the river clears."

"But, still——" He followed me to the kitchen.

I said, "We need some coffee."

We went to bed early, thinking how quickly our lives would change. Through the night John stroked my hair.

"Perhaps we *should* stay, John."

"It's all for the best, Dolly. We've made promises to each other."

When he thought I was asleep he crept cautiously out of bed, lit the lamp and bent over Mae's box bed.

"Is she all right?" I said.

He nodded and came back to me.

"I guess I really didn't think it out before. We've learned a lot in three years. It's taught us to be humble and to appreciate all we've got. I hope our being here has been of help." He got out of bed to blow out the lamp.

Soon the sun would be coming up. Already the river ice was moving. Tomorrow we would watch the geese wheel overhead, and hunt the "fool hen" on the beach as she turned to watch us. Tomorrow, while John finished cleaning and packing the relics to be sent to the Smithsonian, I would take Mae to visit Grace and the other women who had been so kind to her. And tomorrow, as we listened to the river, we would know that during the weeks to come we would welcome the tumultuous roar as the water spread over the tundra. We would watch spellbound; when the river was open, we would leave.

Behind us blizzard-swept trails, the canopy of Northern Lights, the glow of rime on window glass, the red of a timeless sun, the shimmer of the rising moon—and life itself at its most perilous.

John touched my shoulder. "Come back to bed for a while, Dolly."

What I had to tell him could wait another day. Its telling could no longer alter our decision.

"John," I would say softly, "I've been bursting to tell you——"

A waggish reply would be his answer. "And I've been wondering when you would."

I rose to my elbow, looking down at his face serene in sleep. It wasn't something I had to put in words. Even the coin must have known.

Mae, I felt, had been my act of protest against all that was alien in Alaska. Our second child would be a boy, a miniature John, to match his love for this land, for hunting, fishing, for dogs like Kobuk, for guns and the trail, for all I could accept but never need as much as he did.

Our natures were not so very different from the people we'd lived among. In the village we had seen the best and the worst of life, love and cruelty, indifference and sacrifice, communal ties and those who were left to suffer and die alone. Alaska was not simply a land of hardship but a school, a proving ground, a reminder of what in this life is important and what is not. We had gone north toward a shining river—a river we might not have been so quick to challenge and trust at home.

Our second child would be a boy. Let God grant him the courage and determination of his father, the resourcefulness and tenderness which we had learned to admire. Let these years in Alaska be both source and guide to an understanding of men—their differences, their likenesses—and of women too, who followed, steadied, admonished and loved them and who wished their sons no less adventurous.

163   6